The Seventh Edition

of

The How Book For Genealogists

A guide to give the new genealogist a proper start.

A help for the experienced genealogist in the many problems connected with the search for ancestors.

Edited By

GEORGE B. EVERTON, SR.

Published By

The Everton Publishers, Inc.

P. O. Box 368   Logan, Utah 84321

Printed by

Keith W. Watkins and Sons, Inc.
Providence, Utah 84332

FOREWORD

The idea of "The How Book", came to the late Walter M. Everton while he was engaged as an advisor to people interested in genealogical research around San Francisco. He found that scores of inquiries coming to him daily centered around a number of specific topics. Finding he was writing the same kind of letter several times a day in answer to inquiries, he decided to mimeograph each letter he wrote on any particular phase of genealogy. Eventually he had seventy-three different short letters. From two to five of these different letters were sent to each one of the twenty or more daily inquiries. Returning to his home in Logan, Utah, in 1945, he founded the genealogical section of the Cache County Library. When inquiries continued to come from bewildered researchers he decided to combine his letters into a three-and-a-half by eight-and-a-half inch mimeographed, "The How Book For Genealogists." It contained seventy-eight pages. The demand for this little pamphlet was enormous.

The 1948 edition of this work was a letterpress pamphlet, four by seven. "Revised and enlarged" it sold for twenty-five cents per copy. In each new edition additional information was incorporated to provide help to the professional as well as to the amateur researcher. A total of sixteen thousand copies were distributed throughout the nation.

Sensing that more information was needed to guide the researcher than was given in his "How Book," Mr. Everton conceived the idea of "The Handy Book for Genealogists," the first edition of which was printed in 1949. It included, in addition to all the material of the "How Book," a section on "Genealogical Geography," and two other sections, "The Directory of Genealogists" and "The Genealogists's Exchange."

Since 1947 he had also published "The Genealogical Helper" a magazine which was first distributed as a monthly and then as a larger quarterly. Immediately after the publication of "The Handy Book for Genealogists" in 1949 it became obvious to Mr. Everton that the two sections in that book, "The Directory of Genealogists and "The Genealogist's Exchange" were of such tremendous importance to the researcher that they must come out with fresh contents at least once a year. Realizing the impossibility of producing a yearly ten-thousand-copy edition of "The Handy Book," Mr. Everton decided to incorporate those two sections in the quarterly magazine.

He was making preparation for the "First Annual Exchange Edition" of "The Genealogical Helper" in December 1950 when he was stricken by a fatal heart attack.

The 1953 edition of "The Handy Book for Genealogists" was published by The Everton Publishers with George B. Everton, Sr. and Gunnar Rasmuson as editors. It followed the plan of the original "Handy Book" with some additional information and corrections. Next came "The Third Edition of the Handy Book for Genealogists." It did not contain the "Directory of Genealogists" nor the "Genealogists' Exchange." Neither did it contain the general instructions incorporated into this present book, but it had much additional information on the 48 states with a map of each showing county boundaries and much new data on most of the European countries.

The September issue of "The Genealogical Helper," has continued to be "The Annual Exchange Edition" and because of its tremendous growth the March issue of each year will also contain exchange material.

The Fourth Edition of "The Handy Book for Genealogists" was published in 1962. Many corrections were made in this edition and an attempt was made to standardize the "formation date" of counties, using the date of the legislative act rather than the date when the records were started or the officers were elected, as had been done by some authorities of the past. New maps of all the states with their counties were printed in this edition and the counties of bordering states were also shown to assist one in tracing migrations across state lines. Other new additions were "The Genealogists' Check List of Historical Records Survey" and a list of records held by many of the county clerks or clerks of the courts of many counties. The Fifth Edition of the "Handy Book" held to the same format as the Fourth Edition but with many additions. The format of the Sixth Edition published in 1971 was enlarged to 8 1/2 x 11 inches to make possible larger maps and to increase readability of printed material. Again, much new information was incorporated especially data on records held by county officers.

Between 1948 and 1956, while the "How Book" was out of print, seldom a week passed without someone ordering a copy. This continual demand, coupled with new plans and ideas which had been worked out and proven of great help to those interested in genealogical research and the gathering and writing of family and personal histories, finally brought forth the ''New How Book for Genealogists.'' Ten thousand copies were printed and are now in the hands of genealogists all over the world.

In 1959 the ' How Book'' was again revised and updated. It was called the IMPROVED HOW BOOK FOR GENEALOGISTS. This edition was spiral bound and it contained many additional pages. A large amount of improved information was added to aid genealogists in their ''Family Tree Climbing''. Over 10,000 copies of this ediition were again placed in the hands of genealogists all over the world.

As you read this book you undoutedly will find mistakes. You can give a helping hand to us and many other genealogists if you will let us know about these imperfections. Your suggestions and comments will also be welcomed to help us to plan for future editions.

George B. Everton, Sr., Editor

November 1971

INTRODUCTION

Family tree research is one of the most interesting, pleasurable and gratifying hobbies to which you can turn. Following the trails and trials of your forebears can lead you to many exciting tales of successes, triumphs, failures, loves and pathos - true life stories as glamorous as any from Hollywood.

It can also take you to new lands and places, through study and writing, or in person, as you search for the records of your unknown progenitors. You will also broaden your knowledge of history, geography, laws, customs and life in general of the present and the dim past as you delve into records in new and ancient archives.

You will thrill time and time again as you find the accounts of your forefathers' doings - births, marriages, deaths, wills, land transfers, moves, etc. Sometimes you'll run into puzzles as interesting and hard to explain as it is possible to imagine. You will solve some quickly, others may keep you in suspense for years.

How to get started is the big question with

most people. What to do first? How to carry on? Where will I find the records of my people? How and what should I record when I do find them? These questions and many others are answered or explained in THE HOW BOOK FOR GENEALOGISTS. It will start you in the proper way and open hundreds of avenues for you to follow that you may find and record the vital facts and interesting sidelights of your foreparents.

The Everton Publishers have been helping genealogists since before 1947. Besides THE HOW BOOK FOR GENEALOGISTS, they also publish THE GENEALOGICAL HELPER, a bimonthly magazine, THE HANDY BOOK FOR GENEALOGISTS, THE SCANDINAVIAN GENEALOGICAL HELPER and many sheets and forms to help you record your family data.

THE GENEALOGICAL HELPER is published each January, March, May, July, September, and November. It was started in 1947 by the late Walter M. Everton and now has subscribers in every state in the nation and many foreign countries. Thousands have advertised their genealogical problems in its columns and received the solutions from other genealogists who have contacted them after reading the advertisements. Countless unknown, distant cousins of far-away climes have made contact with each other and then corroborated their efforts in their searches for ancestors, through the pages of this widely read ancestral research magazine.

It can help you in your search whether you are just starting or have had a lot of experience in this enchanting hobby. First you should check recent issues to see who might be interested in your lines. Then you should advertise your wants so others will know of your problems and give you assistance.

Reviews of new publications and stories of various genealogical activities are printed in each issue as well as other guides, helps and instructions for all family tree searchers.

The phenomenal growth of this publication attests that it is living up to its dedication "to help more people find more genealogy."

THE HANDY BOOK FOR GENEALOGISTS, now in its sixth edition is probably the most widely used genealogical book ever published. It gives the formation history of every county in the U.S. and much information regarding their vital records. Brief state histories are also given enabling you to know quickly where you might go or write to get information regarding your ancestors.

A map of each state showing its counties as well as the counties of bordering states makes it possible for you to easily trace migrations, one of the inevitables of ancestor research. Much information is also given on most of the Western European Countries, showing you many steps to take in your research across the Atlantic.

You will undoubtedly make this book your constant research companion as thousands of professional and amateur genealogists are now doing around the world.

This, THE HOW BOOK FOR GENEALOGISTS is not only designed to give you a start along the ancestor trail-telling you how to begin and how to continue - but it also has many other helps for the long-time genealogist and the newest neophite. You will find in it a relationship chart as easy to read as a mileage chart, showing kinships to ninth cousins, and a formula to figure relationships as far as you may wish to go. "Cousinships" and "times removed" lose their mystery with the easy to understand explanations given in this widely recognized guide for primogenitor searchers.

Another feature of the "How Book" you will use many times is its Dictionary of Words, Terms and Abbreviations. Here are listed and explained hundreds of seldom understood words and terms, local and foreign, used in recording genealogical data. They are all arranged alphabetically to assist you and save you time. You will use this book as long as you do research on your family tree.

You need GENEALOGICAL FORMS to help you record your findings. The charts and forms from The Everton Publishers will assist you in making your records clear, understandable, convenient to check and add to. They will also aid you in preserving your records for the future and give you justifiable pride and satisfaction when you display them.

Catalogues are available - free of charge - listing all the above and many more instruction books and other aids for genealogical and heraldic enthusiasts. Send for yours now. Just drop a card to: THE EVERTON PUBLISHERS, INC., P.O. Box 368, Logan, Utah, 84321.

TABLE OF CONTENTS

HOW TO BEGIN 1
  Starting your record 6
  Abbreviations may be bewildering . 12
  A family group sheet for each marriage . 13
  Record the truth 16
  Pictures will enhance your record . 18
  Picture pedigrees 24
  Clean old photos 26
  The pedigree chart 27
  Form letters 33
  Listing names on pedigree charts . 35
  Unlimited pedigree record . . . 37
  Family history sheets 42
  Suggestions and items to consider
    in writing your personal history . 44
  Arranging and utlizing your record
    for the greatest satisfaction . . 48
  Why a genealogical record? . . 50
  Write a history 51
  Microfilming 52
  Notes 53, 54
HOW TO CONTINUE 55
  Register your research endeavors . 56
  Suggestions to help solve dis-
    crepancies 58
  Numerous errors 60
  Prove your records 62
  Little equipment needed 63

It takes time to find genealogy . 64
Ask your own family first . . 65
Personal visits are best . . . 68
Prove family traditions 71
Pedigrees must be correct . . . 72
Many people - same name . . . 74
Spell place name correctly . . . 77
Prove all work before continuing . 82
Desired qualities in a researcher . 82
You must write letters 83
Contact persons of similar names . 88
A magazine to help you 89
Where to write for genealogy . . 91
Writing to public officers . . . 93
Use labor saving devices 94
Family genealogists 95
Home town genealogists 96
Write to genealogical libraries . . 97
Printed family histories 98
Library catalogues 102
Borrowing genealogical books . . 103
Records in National Archives . . 104
War records help 106
Census records 107
Naturalization records 109
Passenger lists 110
Land records 114
Introduction to Handy Book for
   Genealogists 117
State histories 119

County histories 120
Libraries 122
Maps 122
County records 123
Genealogists check list of Histor-
  ical Records Survey 124
Early spelling of names 129
Whence came surnames 130
Clues in names 134
Approximating dates 135
Notes 138
RELATIONSHIPS 139
How to use the relationship chart . 139
DICTIONARY OF GENEALOGICAL
WORDS TERMS AND ABBREVIATIONS . 145
  Explanation of terms and symbols . 147
  Genealogical dictionary 151
INDEX 233

I
How To Begin

So you are interested in gathering information about your ancestors. You are not alone with this idea--genealogy is fast becoming a most popular hobby. Lack of tools and instructions on how to use them - such as forms, binders, etc. -have deterred many from taking up this interesting pastime. Gradually, however, these obstacles are being overcome. With the printing of this book one more step has been accomplished to assist those who desire to occupy themselves in this avocation.

As suggested, one of the first things needed is tools with which to work. Many genealogical forms are now available. As these instructions proceed several will be introduced. If you would like a complete set of sample forms (kit 7,8,9) send $1.00 to The Everton Publishers Inc., P. O. Box 368, Logan, Utah 84321. A free catalogue of genealogical supplies will also be sent.

First is the family group sheet. This is the

base or foundation of all genealogical forms. From the information recorded on the family group sheet other necessary genealogical forms can be started and completed. On that sheet, when it is properly done, you have not only the names of your ancestors or relatives, but also the time, place and relationship elements which are almost as essential as the name for proper identification of persons. Many names considered uncommon today may be found in abundance in certain localities in past years. Unless you can connect some dates with those names - tell where and when the persons were born, where and when they were married. where and when they died, and show their relationshp to other persons - their identity is incomplete. It may sometimes happen that with all this information available there may still be a question of being the same person because of conflicting information.

Never be satisfied to gather names only. They may mean something to you today because of your personal acquaintance with the people, but to your descendants in years to come, they will mean nothing without the mentioned identifying particulars.

Thus you can see the importance of the

family group sheet. Different kinds of these sheets are available. Some researchers prefer one kind, others a different kind. As long as it contains the needed information, one kind is as good as another. To satisfy individual desires, The Everton Publishers have available five different kinds of family group sheets, designated as A1, F1, F2, F3, and F6. Different forms may be obtained from other sources. You may find all necessary forms at the store where you purchased this book. They may not have the same designation as given here but they may still be about the same form, with little change. The instructions to be given in these pages almost cover the entire field.

Form A1 is a recent development of The Everton Publishers for forefather searchers who want to use the standard 8 1/2 x 11 inch paper punched for the three-ring binder. It has lines corresponding to the regular typewriter spacing and has spaces for recording more information than most of the forms printed for this purpose. In addition to the usual headings for recording birth, marriage and death dates and places, it also has spaces for occupation, places of residence, church affiliations and military service, etc.

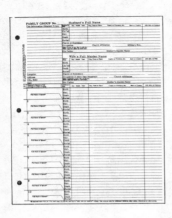

FAMILY GROUP SHEET NO. A-1

Form All (Children Continuation sheet can be used with Form A1 for extra large families. It has spaces for the father and mother (names only) and 14 children (all regular data)

Several other new forms have been printed to be used with the Form A1 in the three-ring binder, including pedigree charts and data work sheets of various kinds. Each will be discussed with their related forms.

Forms F2 and F3, each measuring 8 1/2 x 11 inches, are identical except for the paper on which they are printed. Form F3 is printed on permalife paper. Form F2 is printed on a lighter sulphite paper that may not withstand the ravages of time and turn yellow with age. Since Form F3 is intended for your personal records it is punched to be preserved

FAMILY
GROUP
SHEET
NO. F-3

in a binder.
Form F2, in-
tended mainly
as a work
sheet in prep-
aration for the

long-time-to-be-saved records, is unpunch-
ed. It may also be used in sending or asking
for information from other researchers.

Form F6 measures 8 1/2 x 14 inches and
is punched to fit the regular or deluxe

FAMILY GROUP SHEET NO. F-6

binders. It is printed on permalife paper, as are F3 and F1, but it has more space for recording data.

Form F1 is similar to Form F3 but it measures 8 1/2 x 14 inches and in the extra space are recorded certain ordinances of the Church of Jesus Christ of Latter-day Saints. Members of that church would do well to use the F1, others undoubtedly would prefer the A1, F3 or F6. Form F2 can be used as a work sheet by either group.

Substantial and attractive loose-leaf binders to fit A1, F1, F3 or F6 can be supplied by The Everton Publishers or by most of the stores which sell this book. Many other forms mentioned in these instructions will fit either one or the other of these two binders. You may purchase three-ring binders at any office supply house and most grocery and drug stores. Write to The Everton Publishers for a free catalogue listing the special binders, the above sheets and many other genealogical aids.

STARTING YOUR RECORD

The correct way to gather a genealogical record is to start with your own family.

If you are married, fill in form F2 for the husband, wife and children. This you should be able to do from memory or from recent records made in the family Bible or elsewhere. Each blank is to be filled as if you were doing it for someone entirely unacquainted with your family. If you are not absolutely sure of the dates, don't rely on your memory. (Good genealogists prove every date, place and name with contemporary records, such as birth, marriage and death certificates, Bible, court and census records, old diaries, etc., and they record these sources so they can easily check back and prove every statement or other data they find.) Spell all names correctly. In giving the names of children, list them in order of birth. If a child has died, list its name in the order where it belongs, just as you do for the living children. Use the child's real name -- not a pet name or nickname.

If at all possible, use a typewriter in filling out the record. If a typewriter is not available, print the information in legible style. Don't trust your handwriting -- when it gets cold or is read by a stranger it may be misinterpreted. When writing dates, do it the professional way -- day, month, year -- 10 June 1889. A little time spent in practice along this line may pay big dividends in the future -- both in time and satisfaction.

Write all names in their regular order -- Christian name first, then the middle name if any, and then the surname (John Christian Jones). Be consistent in the style you use for writing names, dates and places, etc., also in the color of ink if you write by hand. Choose a style and stay with it and your record will have more beauty and meaning to you.

Never use initials unless it is impossible to find the name. Rarely will you find someone who was given as his name only initials such as ''R'' ''L'' Smith. In such cases, naturally, you must use the initials, since that's all given. When you record an unusual name, underline it showing that you know it to be correct or in the case of initials for names, place them in quotes (''R'' ''W'' etc.). If a person is widely known by a nickname or a legally assumed or adopted name, it is well to place it within parentheses on the record in connection with the true or original name, as for instance, John (Jack) Jones, Mary (Polly) Smith, Thomas Polk (Paulk), Henry Black (Schwartz). Don't abbreviate names of persons or localities, with the exceptions of the officially accepted abbreviations of states. (See p. 13).

The varied spelling of names is another difficulty you will encounter as you follow your ancestor trails. It is not too unusual to find the name of a person spelled differently each time it is recorded. Illiterate persons had to rely on clerks and other recorders to spell their names. It depended on how the clerk was trained and how the name sounded to him as to how he spelled it. Modern spelling methods also have had their influence on surnames. A good rule to follow in most cases is: Use the spelling of a person's name as you find it in the earliest record of that person. If you find it spelled other ways later and wish to show the changes, place as many different spellings as you wish after the first spelling in parentheses. Of course you may find cases where you will want to deviate from this rule, but show the various spellings to show why you have changed.

On all genealogical records the surnames of females should be the maiden names only. You will avoid a lot of confusion if you adhere strictly to this rule. Regardless of how many times a woman may have been married, use only her maiden name. You will notice there is a space for the names of other husbands she may have had. If her maiden name is unknown, but her given name is known, write, for instance, Mrs. Bertha Cowles, or if the husband's and the children's surname is known and her names are entirely unknown, write it, for instance, Mrs. John Cowles.

After you have completed your immediate family group sheet complete a similar sheet for the family of the husband's parents, then one for the family of the wife's parents. If you have married brothers and sisters complete family group sheets for each of them, being careful that all names and dates are correct. If you are not sure of names or dates call them on the telephone or write to them for the information. Next complete family group sheets for the families of your parents' brothers and sisters. Be just as careful to get all names and dates on those sheets as correct as you were with your own record.

You will find this experience will give you as much satisfaction as any other phase of genealogy. It will also train you in gathering facts and recording them correctly. It will give you a grasp of research activities so that by the time you are ready to prepare the records of your grandparents and great grandparents you'll feel like a professional researcher. You will thus have a better knowledge of what and how to do with more complicated situations as you get into more and more the distant past.

As previously mentioned, a good practice is to write all dates with the day first, then the month and the year. Never indicate the month with a numeral, as 7-12-1893 or 12-7-1893, but always as 12 July 1893. Various parts of the world use different numeral systems as dates and this can lead to confusion and errors. All the months may be abbreviated to three letters with the exception of June and July and they should be written in full. The year should never be abbreviated, as genealogical dates cover all centuries. To eliminate the century and write '95 instead of 1695, or 1795, or 1895 could be perplexing indeed.

The two lines of the form following the name of the husband and wife allow for recording the date and place of birth and the date and place of christening, however, both of these dates are not necessary. The date and place of birth are the most important, although, if they are not obtainable, the christening date and place may be substi-

tuted. In olden days the clergy often neglect-
ed to register the birth of the child, but made
note of the christening date when the child
was brought to the church for that ordinance.
Regarding the time and place of death and
the time and place of burial, it would be
well if you could get all this information.
The death date is the most important but
the burial date and place may give you many
additional clues.

ABBREVIATIONS MAY BE BEWILDERING

Abbreviations of names of persons or localities should be avoided. For instance,
S. A. may stand for South America, South
Africa, South Australia, Santa Ana, Saint Augustine, San Antonio, or San Angelo. While
you know perfectly well what you would have
the initials represent, to all others they
would be an enigma. Your record should
withstand the eye of the critic and the test of
time, therefore, use the full name of the town
or city, the county, province, shire, canton or
lan, fylke, amt, and the nation. States in the
United States may be abbreviated or not abbreviated according to the Postal Guides, as
follows:

Ala.	Ind.	Nebr.	S.C.
Alaska	Iowa	Nev.	S.Dak.
Ariz.	Kans.	N.H.	Tenn.
Ark.	Ky.	N.J.	Tex.
Calif.	La.	N.Mex.	Utah
Colo.	Maine	N.Y.	Vt.
Conn.	Md.	N.C.	Va.
Del.	Mass.	N.Dak.	Wash.
Fla.	Mich.	Ohio	W.Va.
Ga.	Minn.	Okla.	Wis.
Hawaii	Miss.	Oreg.	Wyo.
Idaho	Mo.	Pa.	
Ill.	Mont.	R.I.	

A FAMILY GROUP SHEET
FOR EACH MARRIAGE

In these days of divorces it is not uncommon to find persons who have been married more than once. In the early days, the rigors, dangers and disease of pioneer life often caused homes to be broken by death and the bereaved spouse to secure a new companion. The proper procedure in recording multiple marriages poses problems to the embryo genealogist. However, there is nothing particularly difficult in the situation, if you remember that for each marriage there must be a family group sheet. For each spouse, each husband or wife must have a separate family group sheet on which must be shown the children of that marriage, if any.

Part of the information asked for under the "Husband's Name" on each family group sheet says, "Other Wives, if any." If the husband has only had one wife, that particular line should remain blank. If the husband in question has had the misfortune to lose two wives and has married a third, this notation should be given on that line of the sheet showing the name and data of his first wife. On the line calling for "Other wives, if any", place (2) and the maiden name of second wife; then (3) and maiden name of his third wife. On the sheet showing the information concerning his second wife, that "Other wives" line should read as follows: (1) the name of first wife and (3) with name of third wife. On the sheet showing the information concerning the third wife, that "Other wives" line should read: (1) name of first wife and (2) name of the second wife. Following are examples:

Husband's Name, John Jones
Other Wives, if any, (2) Mary Smith, (3) Jane Roe
Wife's Maiden Name, (1) Anna Brown

Husband's Name, John Jones

Other Wives, if any, (1) Anna Brown, (3)
   Jane Roe
Wife's Maiden Name, (2) Mary Smith

Husband's Name, John Jones
Other Wives, if any, (1) Anna Brown, (2)
   Mary Smith
Wife's Maiden Name, (3) Jane Roe

Thus, with the three sheets you will be able
to record the children of each marriage,
placing them with the proper mother. By
using the proper number in parentheses each
time with each wife's name you eliminate all
questions regarding the wives' order. It may
also be well to place the date of the marriage
between the name and the number -- (2) 16
May 1810 Mary Smith -- (3) 12 June 1816
Jane Roe -- to make sure there is no question as to the order of marriage.

The same procedure in the wife's information should be followed, if she has been married more than once concerning her husbands.

The family group sheet is compiled to help
you remember at a glance the individuals who
are your direct ancestors. In the part where
the children of the family are listed, place an

asterisk (*) in front of the name of your direct ancestors. It naturally follows, of course, that the husband and wife mentioned on that particular sheet are also your ancestors. It may happen that two children on one family group sheet may be your ancestors. For instance, on one such sheet in our possession, the second child became one of our fifth great grandmothers on our mother's side, and the tenth child became one of our fourth great grandfathers on our father's lineage. An asterisk (*) is placed in front of each one of those two names on that family group sheet which includes a total of ten names of children.

How should an adopted child be recorded on the family group sheet? After the names of such a child write (Adopted). If his blood parents are known, list them on the back of the sheet. It would also be well to complete another family group sheet so that his true brothers and sisters may be shown. If the parents are unknown, state that fact. Remember, if possible, blood lines are the ones to follow in tracing genealogy; adopted lines are secondary.

RECORD THE TRUTH

Sooner or later, a majority of those who do

genealogical research find "skeletons in the closet." Some discover illegitimate births or other infractions of the law in their lines. Under such conditions paternity is difficult to prove. Rumors and traditions are poor foundations on which to build a pedigree. There is no need to create a scene, to make unnecessary displays. Better far to be quiet, to forget. However, you have more than likely come to the end of that particular lineage, but there is nothing to hinder you from continuing the search on all other lines. Although it may be unsavory, record the truth, but avoid making it prominent. Don't go into detail about such matters; you will find plenty of things to record of which you will be proud.

Mention has been made that sources of information should be recorded. A space for that purpose is reserved on the front of the family group sheet. If that space is insufficient, list all important data on the back of the sheet. (You may also want to record the number of your Form A4, if you are using this method of compiling your data.) Cross references always help in checking and rechecking records. Many times judgment must be exercised in the interpretation of obscure facts, and your opinion may differ from that of other persons. Give everyone a chance to decide for himself by letting him know the source of your information, such as: Family or Bible records (indicate location of the records); U. S. Census records (name, year, state, county, etc.); family histories (by whom written and published); State Vital Statistics, etc. This is referred to as the "Historical Method". It is a lot easier than the "Legal Method" perhaps, but not so conclusive. (See p. 62).

In the upper right hand corner of the F1, F2 and F6 family group sheets is a place for recording the names of the husband and the wife. As your book grows you will find it convenient to have those names in that position to aid you in locating desired sheets as you thumb through the binder.

PICTURES WILL
ENHANCE YOUR RECORD

One of the most interesting phases of genealogy is the gathering of pictures and mounting them with the family record -- practically bringing the family group alive. This is not too difficult with the living, but the farther back you go on your record the more likely that you will finally reach the time of no photos and portraits. Some researchers have been able to locate pictures for five or six generations on all their lines. When such an array of photographs is added to the family record it is truly a wonderful sight.

Many ways have been devised for sorting, classifying and mounting pictures. To aid you and give you a start, we will discuss a simple method, then you can add to it, change or elaborate on it to your heart's content.

Plain sheets are available for mounting your photos and other material you may want to preserve in your record. The S6 sheet, sold by The Everton Publishers, is 8 1/2 x 14 inches heavy weight bond paper especially made for mounting. The S7 sheet is the same except for measuring 8 1/2 x 11 inches. Both are punched to fit binders. The A8 and A9 sheets are also 8 1/2 x 11 inches but are punched for three-ring binders. The A8 is the same weight as the S6 and S7, and the A9 the same weight as the S4 and S5. Some people have used the S4, S5 and A9 sheets and found them satisfactory, but they are lighter weight, and most people prefer the heavier paper for their permanent records. The lighter weight sheets are used mostly to write histories, other corroborative or interesting material regarding ante-

cedents. As with other sheets, you may find
just what you need at the store where
this book was purchased. You may also be interested in acetate sheets which are used to
cover the mounted pictures or other valuable
records. They may be obtained in the 8 1/2 x
14 inch size, or 8 1/2 x 11 for the three-
ring binders. The added protection and
beauty they give make them well worth their
slight cost.

As with regular recording activities, it is a
good idea to start your picture mounting with
your own immediate family. Place a plain
bond sheet on top of your family group sheet.
Turn the plain sheet over so it will be on your
left as you face it and your family group sheet
is on your right. Paste your family picture on
the plain sheet -- thus when you open your
book after it is assembled you will have your
family group sheet and your picture sheet so
they can be viewed together without having to
turn a page. With ink print the names of the
individuals on the sheet under the picture -
or type them -- in such a way that a stranger
could identify each. Why identify those in the
picture so carefully, since you are intimately
acquainted with them? You'll never forget
who they are! That's true, but twenty-five
years from now and when your descendants

are looking at that picture they may not know any of the people. What wouldn't you give now if grandma had identified pictures by writing the names on the back of each. As it is, there isn't a mark of any kind to identify the photographed person and the picture is worthless to you. Learn a lesson from it. Identify your pictures right now and write the names of each person from left to right, top to bottom. Your descendants will bless you for it! You may also increase interest in the picture by indicating when it was taken and giving other pertinent data about it. You may even have a story regarding the circumstance of its being taken which would add color. If you have several pictures of the family or individuals in question taken at different times arrange them on the same sheet. You may even have enough pictures to fill both sides of the sheet, or you may prefer to use more sheets and mount pictures on one side only. Reserve space for additional pictures you may obtain later. Let us remind you again-- always identify every individual on every picture you use.

Other interesting material may be included such as birth certificates, wedding announcements, marriage licenses, graduation certificates, military service discharge

papers, newspaper clippings, etc., Anything
that is or may become interesting will add
value to your record. You may have some
treasured bits of cloth, locks of hair, old
train tickets, a child's first artwork, old letters, or other material which does not lend
itself to being pasted on the sheet. Paste a
No. 10 or larger envelope on the sheet
and place many of these materials in it. One
word of caution, however, don't make your
family record a scrap book - preserve only
those things pertaining to you personally or
to your ancestors.

A good method for mounting pictures is
that used by professional photographers.
They use what is called photo mounting
tissue --a thin tissue with shellac on both
sides. This is cut to the size of the picture
and placed on the sheet where you desire it;
the picture is placed over it. An electric iron,
warm enough to melt the shellac, is placed
over the picture. It should remain long
enough to melt the shellac, but be careful not
to burn the picture. When cooled, the shellac
hardens and makes a good bond. Photo
mounting tissue in varied sizes may be obtained from photo supply houses. If you use
the acetate sheets to cover your mounted pictures, you need only a small amount of paste

to hold the picture in place. The acetate sheet will give it good protection.

Snapshots as well as formal pictures will add much to your record. The snapshots will give little or no mounting difficulty but some formal pictures may present problems, especially old pictures. For instance, you may find an old group picture of your grandfather's family which is too large to go into your book. It can be copied and reduced to make it usable.

Any professional photographer can do that kind of work. If you are a handy do-it-yourself fellow, prop up the picture somewhere out in the sun, get as close to it as you can with your kodak or cheap box camera and still stay in focus, and shoot the picture just as you would any snapshot. A little experimenting will soon teach you how close you can get and still be in focus. We've seen quite satisfactory results from this method. Those two methods are, perhaps, the extremes in photo copying. Lying between these are the vast resources of the clever amateur photographer with a variety of equipment and devices. Use any method you like but never neglect any opportunity to enrich your genealogical record just because some of the available pictures are not the proper size.

Photo copying also comes in handy when you find a rare old picture and the owner refuses to part with it. Have a copy made of it -- there is absolutely no danger of harming the picture when only ordinary photo processes are used.

PICTURE PEDIGREES

Sometimes you may want a copy of only one person in a group picture. A professional photographer can make the copy of the desired individual in whatever size you may indicate. If you wish to do the work yourself, follow previous instructions. After the print is made you can trim away everything but the part you seek.

Copying one face from a group picture may become a necessity when you are making up a picture pedigree. This is an interesting phase of genealogy. For instance, start with your children, then father and mother, then grandparents and great grandparents and so on back as far as you can go. Form P22 is a picture pedigree sheet for use in our 9x15 inch binders, A6 is designed for the

PICTURE PEDIGREE CHART NO. P-22

three-ring binders. Or you may wish to use plain heavy sheets and arrange the pictures according to your own ideas. We have seen pictures so arranged and then photocopied so that other members of the family may obtain them if they desire.

For your own or close relative picture groups you may want to arrange special sections, such as "Babyhood," "School-days," "Hobbies," "Married Life," "Travels," "Friends" etc. Each section may be divided by the use of separation sheets, which may be decorated with cut-out highly colored flowers and/or as much art work as your ingenuity permits. Guide Sheets for Book of Remembrance to fit the 9x15 inch binders are available from The

Everton Publishers and other supply houses.

CLEAN OLD PHOTOS

Proper cleaning of old photos will enhance their appearance. Quite often they are blotched and dirty. To clean them, dip a cotton pad in "PM Solution" and rub vigorously. "PM Solution" may be purchased at photo supply houses.

Many old photos are mounted on heavy cardboard. To have a copy made, there is no need to disturb the backing; just clean the photo as suggested. If you contemplate mounting the original photo in your book, you will find it can be handled much better if the backing is removed. To do this, insert a sharp knife into one of the corners of the backing and tear away the corner to the back of the picture. Catch the edges along the torn part and continue to tear to the back. Repeat until you have removed enough of the cardboard backing to make the picture pliable and suitable for attaching to the plain sheet. Never try to run a knife or other sharp object under the picture or try to lift it from the backing, as you may ruin it -- the only picture of its kind that is accessible to you. If you have a picture of little value it will be well to do a little practicing before trying a picture of greater value. Using the recommended method will take only about two or three minutes to strip the backing off any old cardboard mounted pictures. After the backing is removed, you may find it desirable to trim the picture to fit to a space on the page or to remove superfluous sections.

THE PEDIGREE CHART

Many people unacquainted with research activities have looked on the pedigree sheet as the most important genealogical record. It does have its place, but in some respects is not so important as the family group sheet. The pedigree chart shows only part of the family records. From the family group sheet comes the information for the pedigree sheet. However, the pedigree chart is a good index of the research accomplishments on direct ancestral lines. In other words, in the pedigree chart you have a record showing direct ascent or descent. It does not show brothers and sisters, but parents, grandparents and great grandparents. Still, brothers and sisters are important factors in the identification of the family, and they are shown on the family group sheet.

After you have done considerable research work and have located most of your ancestors, say to the fourth and fifth generation, your pedigree chart becomes a guide for your future research. The fan-shaped ten generation pedigree chart, Form P12, with spaces for 1022 names of direct

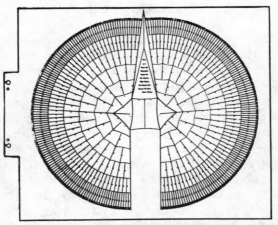

TEN GENERATION PEDIGREE CHART NO. P-12

ancestors, is especially designed for the purpose. If you keep that chart continously abreast with your research, a glance at it

will tell you immediately in which direction
you should devote your research activities.
It measures 22x26 inches, and folds to
8 1/2x14 inches so you can preserve and
keep it ever handy in your binder.

Several kinds of pedigree charts are
available from The Everton Publishers and
other stores carrying genealogical supplies.
The P1, P3 and the P11 are for the 9x15
inch binder. The P1 takes five generations--

PEDIGREE CHART NO. P-1

names of thirty-one ancestors. Each sheet
is arranged so that the pedigree may be
continued for any number of generations
simply by adding more sheets. The P3
measures 14x25 inches but folds into
8 1/2x14 and is punched to fit the 9x15

PEDIGREE CHART
NO. P-3

binder. Eight generations may be listed on the sheet - 255 names. The P11 is 20x25 inches, folds to 8 1/2 x 14 and is also punched for the 9x15 special binder. You may record nine generations - 511 names - on it. Form P2 is a duplicate of P1 but is printed on lighter weight pink paper and is intended only as a work sheet. It can also be used in sending and receiving information through the mail.

Form P7 is a pedigree sheet designed for

PEDIGREE CHART NO. P-7

the 9x12 special binder. It lists five generations -- thirty-one names and has the similar system for extending the pedigree on following sheets as mentioned previously concerning the P1. The P1 and P7 are printed on permalife paper, punched for their respective binders. The P8, a work sheet for the P7, is printed on a light weight sulphite paper and is not punched. Also available for the 9x12 binder is Form P10, 20x25 inches, large enough to handle nine generations.

Form A12, measuring 20 1/2 x 25 1/4 inches, lists eight generations, 255 names. This pedigree chart which has just recently been designed, is for the three-ring binder. It is similar to the P10 and the P11 charts previously described except it is folded to fit the common three-ring binder.

The A2 Pedigree Chart is designed for the three-ring binder. It has spaces for the same number of ancestors (31 names) as the P1 and the same arrangement to extend your pedigree to your most remote ancestor. It will fit into an ordinary typewriter -- all others fit only the wide carriage typewriters. The A24 has spaces for four generations.

ANCESTOR

CHART

NO. A-2

ANCESTOR

CHART

NO. A-24

FORM LETTERS

Most researchers at some time or another have to write for information on a particular phase of their family line to some unknown individual. To many people letter writing is a difficult chore. They take too much time and space to express their need. Form P5 is designed to make

GENEALOGY LETTER PEDIGREE NO. P-5

such a task a most pleasant undertaking. On one side is a short printed letter asking for the needed information with spaces to insert a minimum of words. It has been written by an experienced letter writer using the modern idea that to get the best results, a letter requesting information must take the receiver's point of view rather than the writer's point of view. In other words it is a "you" letter rather than an "I" letter. If you don't care to send a "form letter" for information you might want to use it as a pattern for a personal letter.

On the same side as the letter is a three generation pedigree chart on which the sender notes the names and the relationships of the persons whose data is desired. On the opposite side of the sheet is a four generation pedigree chart to be completed by the receiver of the inquiry and returned to the sender. A lot of time and bother is saved by all concerned by use of this handy sheet. Remember, P5 may save you hours of correspondence!

If you would like more information on how and where to write for genealogical records and data, read the HANDBOOK FOR GENEALOGICAL CORRESPONDENCE, written by the staff of the Cache Genealogical Library, published by Bookcraft, WHAT TO SAY IN YOUR GENEALOGICAL LETTERS, by J. R. Gobble, published by the author, Box 2442,

Idaho Falls, Idaho 83401, also THE HANDY BOOK FOR GENEALOGISTS, published by The Everton Publishers. (see page 235)

LISTING NAMES ON THE PEDIGREE CHARTS

When looking at a pedigree chart for the first time the genealogical novice may feel bewildered and uncertain how to proceed. It should be remembered, first of all, that a pedigree chart is a genealogical tree, a table presenting all known ancestors of person No. 1. Brothers and sisters of one family may be listed in a group as No. 1 on chart No. 1, but all others listed must be parents, grandparents and great grandparents. The name in the No. 1 space on the first chart may be your own, your spouse, your children, your brothers and sisters, your father or mother, or any one whose ancestry is to be traced. If you take one or all of your children for No. 1, it will be your family group pedigree chart, the only one of its kind in the whole world, entirely different from all others. It ties together your family and that of your spouse -- only you and your children can claim it.

Each person has the most important part

of his or her identifying data, such as the full name, when and where born, when married, and when and where died. As in the case of the family group sheet, the married name of women should never appear on the pedigree chart -- always it should be the maiden surname. The abbreviation of names -- even the common ones such as Geo., Thos., Chas., etc. -- should be avoided on the pedigree and the family group sheet. It is well to indicate on the back of the pedigree chart where the data was obtained as mentioned on page 17. Refer to names by their number. The father of No. 1 is placed on line No. 2; the mother of No. 1 on line No. 3. The father of No. 2 becomes No. 4, the mother No. 5. The father of No. 3 becomes No. 6, the mother No. 7. By following this pattern all males will have even numbers and all females odd numbers, with the exception of No. 1 which may be either male or female.

AN UNLIMITED PEDIGREE RECORD

As previously mentioned charts Nos. A2, P1 and P7 are designed to accommodate five generations which can be continued by using additional charts. In using this system, fill out your pedigree on any one line until you come to the fifth generation which is represented by Nos. 16 to 31, inclusive. Indicate in the space provided that the line is continued on chart Number Two. Take your next chart, mark it No. 2 and place the name of the above mentioned person in the No. 1 position. You will also find a space on this sheet which refers back to the previous chart. Fill in the needed information showing that this person (No. 1) is the same person as No._____on Chart No. 1 -- thus giving your reference directions backward as well as forward. Continue on with the pedigree of the above person (No. 1 on Chart No. 2) as far as you can. When you again reach the fifth generation position on Chart No. 2, which of course, would be the ninth generation from the original No. 1, mark the next Chart No. 3. Indicate in the proper places provided on the sheet that this person's pedigree is continued on Chart No. 3 and again make the back reference indicating that person's number on Chart No. 2. Continue this process as far as is necessary to record the information you have gathered on this direct ancestral line. You may then take another line on Chart No. 1 and follow it through in the same manner. It doesn't make much difference which ancestral line you trace first or the order in which they are traced so long as you indicate on each fifth generation name, the number of the sheet which continues that line and that your reference numbers on each chart are correct. The following examples may help you to understand the written directions.

Chart No. 1

1. You - - - - - - - - - -

16. Aaron Brown
Continued on Chart No. 4.

19. Mary Smith
Continued on Chart No. 2.

26. William White
Continued on Chart No. 5.

* *

Chart No. 2
Person No. 1 on this chart is the same person as No. 19 on Chart No. 1

<u>1.</u> Mary Smith — — — — — — — — — <u>24.</u> John Jones
Continued on Chart No. <u>3.</u>

* *

Chart No. <u>3</u>
Person No. <u>1</u> on this chart is
the same person as No. <u>24</u>
on chart No. <u>2</u>

<u>1.</u> John Jones — — — — — — — —

* *

Chart No. <u>4</u>
Person No. <u>1</u> on this chart is
the same person as No. <u>16</u>
on Chart No. <u>1</u>

<u>1.</u> Aaron Brown — — — — — — — <u>16.</u> George Brown
Continued on Chart No. <u>6.</u>

* *

Chart No. <u>5</u>
Person No. <u>1</u> on this chart is
the same person as No. <u>26</u>
on Chart No. <u>1</u>

<u>1.</u> William White — — — — — — — —

* *

Chart No. <u>6</u>
Person No. <u>1</u> on this chart is
the same person as No. <u>16</u>
on Chart No. <u>4</u>

<u>1.</u> George Brown — — — — — — — —

By following this system you can add to your pedigree as the information is gathered -- some today, some tomorrow, and some next year. Pedigrees needing thirty or forty sheets are not at all uncommon. Occasionally some are found with one hundred to several hundred sheets. However, no matter what size it is, it is an easy matter to trace any family line either backward or forward. The important thing is to keep the charts in numerical order and to be sure the reference numbers are correct in both directions.

This method does not show at a glance the whole pedigree as do some of the specially drawn charts. But for permanent records these are more easily handled and better protected in a substantial binder. Each chart has plenty of space with each name for identifying information on each person as to birth, marriage and death. Additional leaves may be added as the lines are extended. Chart forms A2, A24, P1 and/or P7 lay the foundation for any special pedigree chart you may wish to construct, and assist you in organizing your research campaign.

Under ordinary circumstances only blood

lines should be followed on the pedigree chart. However, if you do find foster parents on your lines and wish to trace their ancestry because it is impossible to connect to the blood line, clearly indicate on your chart that they are foster parents. Record the truth -- nothing else will stand the test of time.

As you become more acquainted with genealogical books and charts you will find some very complicated pedigree charts. Almost every one of these has been arranged in a special manner to show special connections. None of them shows all the ancestors which might have been found as can be shown when using the above system. To make an explanation of the construction methods used to draw up these special pedigrees would take considerable space and would be of little value as each one would require special treatment and they are all different. Don't worry about them until you have to, if ever, then get an expert to help you if you can't figure them out for yourself. Simplicity and completeness are embodied in the system using Forms A2, A24, P1 and P7 more than in any other system we are acquainted with.

FAMILY HISTORY SHEETS

Genealogy and history are closely connected. In many ways they compliment and assist each other. In fact, it is difficult to separate them. Genealogists have learned it is well to keep a record of historical facts pertaining to family members. It enriches the family record, preserves notable family deeds, unites more firmly family members, freshens family traditions, assists in the identification of family members, and, above all, adds interest to the genealogical record.

Often, when in a meditative mood, you have chuckled inwardly as almost forgotten incidents have passed in review before your inner eyes. If they were known to your children or children's children wouldn't they cause them to chuckle, too? And, yet, when someone suggests to you that you should write a history of your life, you shrug your shoulders with the comment, "Oh, nothing of importance ever happened to me. My life is just a dreary repetition of uninteresting events." You had better discard that notion right now. If you don't use a typewriter, you had better take your pen in hand and write some of the things you can

remember from your childhood and courtship days. As you get started, you will be
surprised over the many incidents that come
rushing through your mind. Your pen can't
keep up with the onrushing memories of by-
gone days. If you have a son or daughter or
other relative proficient in shorthand tell
your stories to one of them. It would be
better if the two of you were in a room alone,
where nothing could disturb or interfere with
you. In an hour you would have quite a bit
of fascinating history. You could repeat
that every day or so for a month or longer
and you would have a priceless history to
leave with your posterity.

If any member of your family has one of
the recording machines, which are now in
vogue, you may merely tell your story to it.
Before starting to dictate a record you
should make a draft or outline of the things
you expect to talk about.

Family history sheets are available from
most genealogical supply houses. S1 measures 8 1/2x14, S2 and A3 8 1/2x11, all are
ruled and punched on permalife paper. It is
a good practice to place the family history
sheet following the family group sheet --
then with the pictures facing the front of the

family group sheets and the history on the back, the record of one family is complete.

SUGGESTIONS AND ITEMS TO CONSIDER IN WRITING YOUR PERSONAL HISTORY

1. Your birth: when, where, parents, surrounding circumstances and conditions.

2. Your childhood: health, diseases, accidents, playmates, trips, associations with your brothers and sisters, unusual happenings, visitors in your home, visits to grandparents, relatives you remember, religion in your home, financial condition of parents.

3. Your brothers and sisters: names, date of birth, place of birth, accomplishments, names of spouses, date and place of marriage, their children.

4. Your school days: schools attended, teachers, courses studied, special activities, associates, achievements, socials, report cards, humorous situations, who or what influenced you to take certain courses or do things you might not otherwise have done.

5. Your activities before, after and in between school sessions: vacations. jobs, attendance at church, other church functions, scouting, sports, tasks at home, fun and funny situations.

6. Your courtship and marriage: meeting your spouse, special dates, how the question was popped, marriage plans, the wedding, parties and receptions, gifts, honeymoon, meeting your in-laws, what influenced you most in your choice of spouse.

7. Settling down to married life: your new home, starting housekeeping, bride's biscuits, spats and adjustments, a growing love, making ends meet, joys and sorrows, your mother-in-law, other in-laws.

8. Your vocation: training for your job, promotions, companies you worked for, salaries, associates, achievements, your own business.

9. Your children: names, dates and places of birth, health of mother before and after, how father fared, characteristics, habits, smart sayings and doings,

growing up, accomplishments, schooling, marriage, vocations, sicknesses, accidents, operations.

10. Your civic and political activities: positions held, services rendered, clubs, fraternities and lodges you have joined, military service record.

11. Your church activities: as a young person, through adolescence, churches attended, church positions, church associates, church certificates, answers to prayers, necessity and power of love.

12. Your avocations: sports, home hobbies, dramatic and musical activities, reading habits, genealogy, travels, favorite songs, movies, books, writers, poems, etc.

13. Special celebrations or holidays you remember: Easter, Christmas, national and local holidays, vacations.

14. Your plans and hopes for the future.

15. Your ancestors: your impressions of those you knew personally: a general

sketch of those you did not know;
father, mother, grandparents, great
grandparents, and other relatives.

16. Your encouragement and counsel to
your descendants: carrying on family
traditions and activities; their obli-
gations to their country, church and
family; your suggestions to your progeny and others on honesty, humility,
health, diligence, perseverance, thrift,
loyalty, kindness, reverence, the Bible
and other edifying books; service to
fellowmen; your belief regarding God,
etc.

Never underestimate the effect you
may have on unborn generations in
helping them through the trials and
tribulations of life by the written word
of advice you leave your children,
grandchildren, etc. If you would like
them to live upright honest lives, give
them the benefit of your experiences.
Job, of the Old Testament, lamented
the fact that his words were not
written when he said, "Oh that my
words were now written! Oh that they
were printed in a book! That they were
graven with an iron pen and lead in the
rock forever!" (Job, 19-23) But they

were written, and he then gave his beautiful testimony of the Redeemer which has been used countless times as the text of sermons in both the Jewish and the Christian worlds. Your communications to your descendants must be written. They will also appreciate your life story as a precious treasure, and bless you all their days for it.

17. Hints on writing your life story: tell your story plainly and with directness; write truthfully of uplifting, refined and honorable occurrences and experiences. Humor helps to make for easier reading. If you can give the whys of your decisions and changes in activities it may help others. Illustrate with as many pictures as possible. Make several copies, or better still, mimeograph or print and give one to each of your children and grandchildren. Place copies in local and national libraries and/or historical societies.

ARRANGING AND UTILIZING YOUR RECORD FOR THE GREATEST SATISFACTION

Many advantages will be gained by using loose leaf sheets and binder for the preservation of your valuable records. You can add to your book at will or re-arrange it as you may desire any time. You may find additional historical facts or discover some valuable pictures which you want to add to your collection. You can make such changes any time you desire. Additions to living families, new marriages or deaths can be added as they occur. The place for recording these events is the family group sheet. The time for recording these events is immediately after they have occurred while it is still on your mind. "A stitch in time saves nine."

In putting your book together some order is necessary if you are to locate with ease the sheets you have compiled. Many have found it a good idea to place the pedigree sheets in the front of the book followed by their own family group pictures, record and history. After this they place the records of their married children, if any, and then the records of all ancestors and relatives in alphabetic order, using the husband's surname as a guide. If you find several husbands with the same surname, arrange them according to their age, the eldest first and so on. If a husband has had more than one wife, place wife No. 1 first, No. 2 second, and so on.

WHY A GENEALOGICAL RECORD?

It is a real honor to claim descent from pioneer ancestors. Many have traced their lines to progenitors who landed on the bleak shores of New England on November 20, 1620. Descendants of that brave band now belong to "Society of Mayflower Descendants." It was organized in December 1894 to preserve the memory, the records, the history, and all the facts relating to the "Mayflower" Pilgrims, their ancestors and their posterity. All lineal descendants of the original pilgrims are qualified for membership.

Many societies have grown out of the desire to honor the memory of those stalwarts who fought for the independence of our nation. "The National Society of the Daughters of the American Revolution," (DAR), and the "National Society of the Sons of the American Revolution," (SAR), two of the largest, have thousands of members proud of the part their ancestors played in the establishment of our beloved country.

All of the original colonies have similar societies, all of them dedicated to honoring the memory of the originators. Those desiring membership in these patriotic organizations must prove their eligibility with an authentic pedigree showing their descent from the claimed ancestors.

Your genealogical record will form the basis of the record necessary to join many of these organizations. You will be proud to prove that on your family tree are some who helped lay the foundation for this nation or performed other notable deeds worthy of unceasing praise.

WRITE A HISTORY

Another use for the information you may gather and assemble in your genealogical record is as a basis for a printed book honoring the memory of your ancestors -- giving their history and recording their descendants. Recognizing a great truth, Daniel Webster said, "He who careth not from whence he came, careth little whither he goeth." Your vision will be focused on the future by seeking the records of and venerating those who gave you your heritage. You are looking ahead by looking back.

MICROFILMING

It may be that you will not be prepared to publish a book after your work of assembling your loose-leaf record, yet you recognize that something should be done to preserve it for generations to come. In such cases, you may find microfilming the solution to your problem. By this method your record can be put on a small roll of film at a small cost. If you take your record to a genealogical library they may be willing to make a copy for their own use at no cost at all to you. In most large cities are companies who make a business of microfilming. Look in the classified pages of the telephone book if you desire their services. A few microfilm copies placed strategically with genealogical libraries would assure the preservation of your records for all time.

But, what if you neither want it published or microfilmed? Well, the personal satisfaction of having compiled the record ordinarily compensates for all the time, effort and money expended in the pursuit of your family tree and the record of your relatives. It is a fascinating hobby, delving into history, geography, court records, church records -- on familiar ground as well as foreign places. It has been reduced to a science and is now taught in many schools in many parts of the world. Once it is started, it is difficult to abandon. But it should be done right to derive the greatest pleasure. You will be on the right tract if you follow the instructions in this book. Practice will eventually lead to perfection.

NOTES

II
How To Continue

Genealogy continues to attract more and more people as devotees of this extremely interesting pastime. Ancestral information is gathered every year with accelerating impetus. And with this growing activity of searchers comes an impulsion to record keepers, private and public, to assist by making more records available. Advanced printing and copying devices have also helped to make antecedent hunting much easier than in former times. Every year sees hundreds of new genealogy books and other printed aids in the hands of those who are desirous of extending their knowledge of their parental and collateral lines.

Genealogy is not easy to find: it still requires lots of ingenuity and long hours and months of diligent study. A sincere researcher never gets discouraged although it takes a lot of work, he knows success seldom comes without planned and applied effort. If one method fails, another is tried until the needed information is finally found.

The suggestions that follow should be read and reread time and again since it is difficult to retain everything read in one sitting.

REGISTER YOUR RESEARCH ENDEAVORS

One of the difficulties genealogists find as they proceed with their research endeavors is that they make searches of certain records and make no notations of these searches. Then after a lapse of time they forget what and where they have searched and turn again to the same sources, distinctly a waste of time. To help eliminate this trouble many of the serious researchers have taken to making a log or register of all their searches. Every time they engage in any research activity they make a short record of it; the date; the name of the book or record; a brief statement of results.

To assist those who desire to make such a register, The Everton Publishers have made available a form called "Research Register", A5. It advises that you number your searches as well as date them. Also that you transfer the number of the search to the record you make of that search, such as the family group sheet, the form A4 (a description of which follows) or other re-

RESEARCH

REGISTER

SHEET

NO. A-5

DATA

WORK

SHEET

NO. A-4

cord. Then if questions arise you may quickly refer from the register to your record or vice versa to check any point you wish. It may save you a lot of time later if you make such a register of your quests for ancestor material.

In connection with your "register" you may also want to start a system of filing the old letters, birth, marriage and death certificates, copies of wills and other court records, etc., which you may gather as you glean forefather facts. A good system used by many is very simple. Just take a common 14 inch file folder and use prong fasteners to secure to the folder each certificate, old letter, photo copy or other piece of evidence you might gather. This is a system used by most lawyers and business firms to preserve valuable letters, etc. Supplies for this may be purchased at any office supply house. Number each piece consecutively as you fasten it in the folder and register that number on your A4 forms and also on your permanent record to give you quick reference as to where it is filed if ever you need it for further study.

SUGGESTIONS
TO   HELP   RESOLVE   DISCREPANCIES

As you start recording the names, dates and places regarding your relatives and ancestors you will find that not all records agree in the data they reveal. Dates may vary, names may be spelled differently, places and relationships may not correspond. This is extremely disconcerting to the beginner. To help to resolve this difficulty you should first record word for word and letter for letter (verbatim and literatim) the information you find on each record, and state where you found the data. This can be easily accomplished by using Form A4 which has spaces provided for most categories of facts used in genealogical records. It also has spaces for indicating various types of records making it possible for you to just check ☑ your source.

After you have searched all records available regarding this person you may lay out all your form A4's on him and easily make comparisons. In some cases you may want to use a discrepancy chart and put all the information in question on one sheet in columnar form to make it even more handy to compare and check.

Then comes the task of deciding which record is correct and which is incorrect. A good rule to follow, though it is not always true, is that the record that was made nearest to the date of the event is the one most likely to be correct. For instance, a date of birth from a parish record is much more likely to be right than one taken from a census record. Or, a marriage date taken from a marriage certificate undoubtedly would be more acceptable than one from a personal history written years after the event. A death date on a tombstone erected years later should not have the weight given an old letter recorded a few days after the death. The place of birth recorded in a biography would more than likely be erroneous if it disagreed with a birth certificate.

NUMEROUS ERRORS

Just because you find an event written in a book or even in several books doesn't always make it a fact. Many an error has been copied and recopied over and over again. Printed records are excellent sources for clues but unless the author has documented his facts or has given references as to where he obtained his material, be careful. It may be that he has reproduced errors of others or made mistakes of his own. And though he has documented and referenced his book, it would still be well for you to test his sources to be sure he has not erred in his judgment or transcriptions.

Original, official records usually are the most reliable sources for genealogical information -- contemporary recordings in most cases would be considered next best -- then the records made after the event. But, this does not hold in all cases.

The official cemetery record of Isaac Gaisford gave 1875 as his birthdate (he died in 1890), but all other unofficial records gave 1815 as his birth. As he had married twice before 1875, had immigrated to America in 1852, had 12 children, and had been recorded in other unofficial contemporary records long before 1875, that date had to be discarded for 1815. It can be easily seen how the seven could have been substituted by the recorder for the one to make this error.

Poor memories, mistakes in copying, as well as intentional deceptions have caused countless errors in records, making it necessary to check as many sources as possible and weigh all the evidence before making a decision as to which is right. Much more information can be found regarding evaluating records in Derick Harland's "Genealogical Research Standards" published in 1963 by Bookcraft, Salt Lake City, Utah. It is available at most genealogical supply houses.

PROVE YOUR RECORDS

The satisfaction of a job well done comes only by doing the job at hand properly. If you want the most from your genealogical activities use the methods which long experience has found to be the right methods. Avoid errors by correctly copying names, dates and places. Proofread carefully everything you have written. Prove all data and indicate how and where you have proved it.

In the past many researchers have failed because they have taken too many things for granted which later were proved wrong. Just because you read something in a book or a newspaper, don't take for granted that it is true. Prove it before you make it a permanent part of your record. And when you have proved it, show where the information was obtained, so others also may be sure of its correctness. The novice may say, "Well, all of that is easy to say, but how is it done?" A substantial portion of the expert genealogists use the legal method to prove their records -- they have photostatic or certified copies of birth, marriage and death certificates, wills, etc. to prove every step or point in their records. Some consider this is not necessary. They deem it sufficient to indicate where the information was obtained which is commonly called the historical method.

The large majority, however, probably use a combination of both methods, documenting their evidence where possible and citing their references otherwise. Choose which method you prefer but be sure you do not fail to indicate where or from whom you gained your information as you record it. If you don't, you may forget and then later on wish that you had noted your source. Using the A4 "Data Work Sheet" and the A5 "Research Register" will help if not entirely eliminate this difficulty of wondering where you obtained your data when you want to check it.

LITTLE EQUIPMENT NEEDED

If you are just beginning your genealogical

research activities, you don't need to load yourself down with a lot of equipment. All you need is a ten cent notebook or a few, Form A4, data work sheets (which may be a valuable help in guiding you in what to seek or ask for to record your findings.) If you are going to call on some relatives for whatever information you can pick up, you may take along a fountain pen, if you desire. But you should remember that most libraries prohibit the use of ink when copying from their books because if the pen leaks there is a chance some of the printed words may be completely obliterated. The most important part of your "equipment" is an inquisitive mind, a pleasant attitude, and a knack for asking questions.

IT TAKES TIME TO FIND GENEALOGY

The suggestions offered here may help you find some of your ancestors. Again, they may bring you no results. No one can tell for sure where you can find genealogy. The best anyone can do is to suggest where you may find it. If you hire a professional genealogist, he will search where he thinks your records are. Regardless of how careful he may be, he will find nothing if your records are not there. No reliable genealogist ever guarantees to find any particular record unless he definitely knows it is there. Hence, you should not feel discouraged or cancel the search should you have the experience of paying for a search that brings no returns.

Likewise, you may write thousands of letters without results. Most of them may never be answered and others have nothing to tell you. Many family events, such as marriages, births, and deaths were never recorded where one would expect the records to be. If you fail to find them at once, don't quit, but try the harder. Undoubtedly they were recorded somewhere, and eventually you will find the records, even if it should take years. By following the suggestions recorded here many people have found the desired results.

ASK YOUR OWN FAMILY FIRST

It is not at all uncommon for the beginner in research activities to spend time and money in genealogical pursuits only to find that other members of the family have already searched and found the same names. To avoid such unnecessary waste of time and means always start your research in your own family. Here are some questions to which you should have the answers before going too far into your research.

1. Is some other family member searching for genealogy on your branch of the family?
2. What family member has more genealogical data than you have?
3. Does any branch of the family own an old family Bible containing any genealogical information?
4. Does any family member have in his possession copies of gravestone inscriptions in old, forgotten family grounds?

If yours is a large family scattered over many states, it may require many letters and more months to get the needed information. Besides uncles and aunts, you should write to cousins of the third, fourth, and fifth degree, as well as first and second cousins, and in-laws who may have records and information of some of your dead relatives.

"Ten Basic Steps in Genealogy" published by the Genealogical Society of the Latter-Day Saints Church lists 8 points to consider when you write a letter.

1. Letters should be CLEAN and ATTRACTIVE in appearance. Don't write in pencil or with red, green, or purple ink. A typewritten letter or one written clearly and legibly in black or blue-black ink on a clean sheet of paper will go a long way in creating a good first impression.
2. BE COURTEOUS! Don't demand information. Ask for the assistance of the person to whom you are writing. Enclose a stamped, addressed envelope for the reply.
3. BE CLEAR! If the reader doesn't fully understand what you want, he can't possibly send it to you. Don't leave what you want to the imagination of the recipient. Ask for what you want in plain language.
4. BE CONCISE! Don't assume that the reader will "plough" through page after page searching for one request item. Be brief!
5. BE HELPFUL! Make your letter easy to read and easy to answer. If you are asking for several items, number your requests 1, 2, 3, etc. Itemizing your requests will make your letter easier to answer.

6. BE REASONABLE--DON'T ASK FOR TOO MUCH AT ONE TIME! Don't expect persons who have been active in genealogical work for years to send you a copy of all the pedigree charts and family group records in their possession. To satisfy such a request could involve weeks, even months of copying, and so offer to do any copying involved.

7. OFFER TO SHARE WHAT GENEALOGICAL INFORMATION YOU HAVE! If a relative is aware that you will pass on what information you have there is a better chance of his sharing with you.

8. PLAN YOUR LETTER CAREFULLY! Write an outline first, then a rough draft. Next go over it item by item before preparing the final letter.

Letters reveal your character, your personality, just as do your face and actions. Since you desire to make a good impression on the persons from whom you are seeking family information, you should be careful that the looks and the tone of your letter represent you precisely as you would want to present yourself personally to these individuals.

PERSONAL VISITS ARE BEST

Letter writing is a good way for you to gain the needed information, but personal visits are far better. Most people would rather talk than write. That's why thousands of letters go unanswered. If your grandparents or other older members of your family, like brothers or sisters of any of your grandparents, live even two or three hundred miles away, it could pay you in the long run to visit with them.

Many experienced researchers spend their vacation periods doing research work in the community where their grandparents or great grandparents lived. They visit not only with relatives but with former neighbors or intimate associates of their ancestors, most of whom generally have something worthwhile to add to the data desired. On-the-spot research generally is productive of a wealth of information.

To be a successful genealogist you must be a willing listener. You must train yourself to ask short, direct questions, and then listen intently to the, perhaps, long drawn-out story of the interviewed relative. Keep your notebook handy while he is talking with you. As you listen, carefully select from his story the points of value and interest you need for your records. Write them in your notebook while he is talking. If dates and names are given, be sure to write them correctly, being careful to get the right spelling of names and places. Don't take anything for granted. Whenever you're in doubt, ask questions and record the answers.

If the person has any old family Bibles or records, ask permission to see them. Copy from them whatever valuable family information they may contain. Record the births, marriages, deaths, etc. Also the date the Bible was printed and whether the writing in it appears to have been recorded all at one time or at different times, such as, near the time of each event. Old Bible information is wonderful but is is much more acceptable if the record is contemporary with the occurence. So it is with all other records -- the greater the lapse of time between the event and the recording of the event the greater the chance of error.

Don't be satisfied with information received from one relative or a single source. Contact other family members and relatives and compare the information they give you with what you have already gathered. Never discard any information until you are sure it is wrong. "Genealogical Research Standards" by Dereck Harland, published by the Genealogical Society, 107 South Main St., Salt Lake City, Utah 84111, will assist you in evaluating your records. It is also an excellent book to assist you to save time in your research by showing you how to organize and proceed to solve your problems.

PROVE FAMILY TRADITIONS

Tradition is a statement, opinion or belief, or a body of statements or opinions or beliefs, that has been handed down from age to age by oral communication, without the aid of written memorials. Many families have traditions that have come down from earlier days. In olden times there were no movies, no theaters, no radio, no television. During the long, dark nights of those years, the family gathered around the fireplace watching the burning logs. Older family members told and retold stories about the family ancestors and their accomplishments. Those stories grew with each telling and eventually developed into traditions to which the family has clung as valuable mementos. Some of these traditions are true. Others are based on inaccuracies and the more vivid imaginations of the story tellers.

Never embrace any family tradition with too much enthusiasm. Search, investigate and prove every pretended relationship with men of high estate -- statesmen, barons, nobles or royal family members. Carefully trace the tradition to its origin and it may appear more drab and commonplace than it did after years and years of industrious applications of an imaginary lustrous tint, continuously polished by an over-inflated ego. However, if the tradition is founded on fact, you may be able to extend that particular family line on your pedigree chart for several generations since such families have usually maintained printed genealogies for many centuries.

PEDIGREES MUST BE CORRECT

An accurate genealogy is priceless. Diligence is the price paid for accuracy. All source material must be thoroughly searched and weeded. If the remaining material is complete it can be woven into an accurate family record. Just to scan the source material will not insure an accurate record.

Accuracy is of prime importance. Even

though it may take a longer time, it will bring a lasting satisfaction. By employing all available sources of information errors can be eliminated and the work done well.

Every pedigree delineation must be based on facts. One little mistake may invalidate months of research on a wrong line. Too often tradition is built on misinformation and hearsay. Let us caution you again to check carefully all rumors or traditions before you start to incorporate them into your pedigree. Some people have the false notion that anything appearing in print is correct. The person who prepared the material for printing may have built the article on a wrong premise or even if he was correct, the typesetter or the proofreader may have made an error. While reporters and newspaper workers don't make mistakes deliberately, sometimes they may be careless. In checking an obituary in an old newspaper, we found three glaring mistakes in one name. That's poor proofreading!

We have seen beginners in research extend an already started pedigree. They failed to check on the accuracy of the data given. They were unaware of the fact that the person who had started the chart had jumped to conclusions and results had entered names and other data entirely foreign to that pedigree. Naturally all of that work was worthless and had to be discarded. Several months of hard work had to be eliminated.

MANY PEOPLE - SAME NAME

There are thousands of persons with exactly the same name. In checking a name file in a genealogical library, we found nine hundred different individuals bearing the name of Nils Rasmusson, all of them born at different times and different localities in Sweden. In one community we knew two men bearing the name of William West. One of them lived in the east part of town, the other in the west. To distinguish them the townspeople called one of them William East. But fifty years from now if the researchers are looking for them they will find both of them on the records as William West.

A woman in an adjoining state wrote us to help her find one of her husband's ancestors by the name of Christopher Black who came from Germany to Maryland before the Revolutionary War. In reading her letter we thought, "There never was a German man with the name of Black." We checked several early records but were unable to find a Christopher Black, but when we followed our hunch on reading the letter, we found a Christopher Schwartz, (meaning black in German), who had been named an Ensign in the armed forces supplied by Maryland for the war.

There are in America many Nelson families who originated in Sweden. Should you look for them in Sweden remember that the name is Nilsson. Many families coming from various countries of Europe have Americanized their names after being here for a while. Be sure to take that into consideration when you are looking for your ancestors in their original habitat. Many of these foreign descendants know little or nothing about their mother tongue. They have only their names, perhaps wholly or partially anglicized, to remind them that their background is different from those of their neighbors.

Also, be sure to consider the possibility of a different spelling of any name if you have difficulty in extending your lines. Prior to the 20th century comparatively few people could spell their own names. They had to rely on the priest, the clerk of the court, the tax collector or other recorders to do the spelling for them. It is not unusual to find one person for whom the records of the church spell his name one way, the court another way, the census another way and the vital statistics still another way. He pronounced his name to the recorder in each case -- the recorder wrote it as it sounded to him. If the recorder had English training he wrote it the English way. If he was of French origin he brought the French influence into the spelling. In one case a family had been known by, the name of DeMille for several generations in Dutchess County, New York. They moved to New Jersey and the pastor of the Reformed Dutch Church recorded their names as Vandermilt, reverting to the Dutch custom. And so it is with practically every name -- you don't have to go very far back to find it spelled differently -- sometimes entirely.

It would be well for you to record on your Form A4, or other notebook, the various spellings of each person's name exactly as you find them. Then when you make up your family group record use the earliest spelling as the main spelling but place the other spellings in parentheses following the name to assist in further research problems.

As you add names to your pedigree, identify them with the names of the places in which they were born and died, also the dates of birth, marriage and death. If your family group sheets are complete, this should be an easy matter. (See pages 6, 129).

SPELL PLACE NAMES CORRECTLY

Most obituaries of foreign born persons printed in American newspapers contain wrong or misspelled place names. The reason may be something like this: Grandma came from Europe before her teens. She could speak her native language, but couldn't spell. If and when anyone wanted to make a record of her birthplace, it was written as it sounded to the American-trained ears of the writer when Grandma pronounced it. In most cases it was misspelled. Sometimes the spelling is so corrupt it is impossible to find the correct interpretation. The correct spelling of place names are of tremendous importance. Gazetteers are very useful in this connection. If your library does not have those you need, you may be able to get the ones you want from a lending library.

Another way to help untangle twisted up place names is to contact natives of those countries involved. Many American cities have residents from almost every nation. Go to one of those born in Grandma's country and have him help you determine the correct spelling of her birthplace. He may feel honored you came to him for assistance.

Some American-born children of European parents have the erroneous idea that more dignity comes to the family if their ancestors came from the capital of their native land. Thus, when the birthplace is unknown to them, they sometimes add in explanation, "It was near Oslo, or Berlin, or Stockholm, or Amsterdam, or Copenhagen, or London, or Paris, or Bern." And this occurs, even though the place may be hundreds of miles from the capital. Such a statement muddles instead of clarifies the situation.

Let us repeat to emphasize a serious situation. Many pedigree charts contain incorrect place names and some of these errors come from faulty spelling. Ridiculous mistakes occur when names are spelled as pronounced, and often the pronunciation is entirely wrong. This is true not only in case of foreign place names but of American place names also. In other cases carelessly written records have been miscopied time and again. Sometimes the names of an estate, farm or of little neighborhoods are given which are neither post offices nor churches. The post office name may be correct, but it may be connected with the wrong county or state. Even names of rivers, canyons or lakes are given instead of the post office or parish. In some European countries there are towns and localities in thirty or forty different parts which bear exactly the same name. For that reason it is necessary that the name of the particular county accompany the name of the locality. The same holds true in the United States. For instance, there is a Glenwood in each of at least twenty states in the union. Most of us know that Maine and Oregon each have a Portland, but how many know there are Portlands in each of fourteen other states. The same holds true with every nation in the world, no doubt. To differentiate between localities we must have the town or city, the county, and the state or country. Otherwise you would not be able to pursue your genealogical research correctly. You may be

able in each of those counties to find
families of your surname, but it is doubtful
if any but those in the correct county or
nearby counties would belong to your ancestors.

Since these designations of town and
county are different in the various languages, we present herewith a list of them to
make your research work lighter:

State or Country	County	Town or City
Denmark	amt	by or stad
England	shire or county	borough or city
Finland	laani	kyla, kauppala or kaupunki
France	departement	village or ville
Germany	kreis	ort, dorf, or stadt
Iceland	sysla	sokn, baer
Ireland	shire	borough, city
Netherlands	provincie	dorp, stad
Norway	amt or fylker	by, sogn, stad
Scotland	shire	registration branch or city
Sweden	lan	by, koping, stad
Switzerland	bezirk, kanton	dorf, stadt
Wales	swydd	pentre, terf, dinas

Be extremely careful that your pedigree
chart is correct. If the personal names are
known but the place names are unknown or
wrong, it is impossible to do effective research. When errors are located in your re-

cord, be sure to correct all copies, so that the old error will not be recopied.

The dates should also approximate those belonging to other individuals in the similar brackets on the chart. That is to say, there should not be too great a variance in the birth and the marriage dates of the four grandparents, the eight great grandparents, etc.

Other mistakes commonly found in genealogical records which have not been carefully checked include the following: death date prior to marriage or birth of a child; marriage date within a few years of birth date; marriage dates of two wives (or husbands) not consistent; children's birthdates not conforming with age of mother; children's birthdates too close together; father's military record too early or too late in life; and the like. Too much spread between the ages of husband and wife should also be checked very closely - it may be correct but it is unusual. It is a wise procedure to examine all dates and compare them with the rest of your record to see that they are all consistent and reasonable. If they are not, find out why.

PROVE ALL WORK BEFORE CONTINUING

You can't be reminded too often to extend an already started pedigree chart you should first be sure to prove the work already done. Before you extend such a chart, you should be able to answer two questions: "Who placed this name on the chart?" and "How did he know it is correct?"

The same is true with most other records which may come into your hands. If possible have legal proof - evidence that will stand up in court - for every step up your ancestral ladder. This is not always possible, but, you should make it a rule to try every avenue to legally prove every name, date and relationship on your chart. Then you will be a real genealogist.

DESIRED QUALITIES IN A RESEARCHER

Donald L. Jacobus, one of America's foremost genealogists, in his highly instructive book, "Genealogy as Pastime and Profession," says, "The genealogist should possess certain natural aptitudes, sharpened by experience. He should be painstaking, thorough, and accurate. He should be able to weigh evidence; to assemble in logical order a host of details; to construct hypotheses and test them. He needs the detective instinct, and experience must have taught him which of several clues is most likely to lead him to his object. He needs imagination, toned down by long training, and directed by sound reasoning. Especially he needs an excellent memory. Granted this natural equipment, much study and special knowledge are essential.

"A genealogist should not be opinionated, but should always keep an open mind and be ready to admit, on occasion, that his first conclusion was a mistaken one. Those who fear that admission of error will damage their professional reputations as genealogists will not suffer much from any admission. Adherence to truth is more important than professional pride."

YOU MUST WRITE LETTERS

Making personal visits in search of your genealogical data is undoubtedly the best method, but also the most expensive. Some letters must be written eventually to bring together the needed information. Whether you live in a remote part of a desolate country section or adjacent to the largest library in a populous city, letter writing brings good returns to the researcher. Not many people are inclined to letter writing. It is a chore they hesitate to undertake and therefore put off as long as they can. That is the reason so many of the letters you send out go unanswered.

In writing your letters never mention anything about religion or politics. That may stir up a hornet's nest. Hundreds of thousands of American families today are genealogically minded. Hence, it is absolutely unnecessary for you to tell why you are compiling your genealogy. Nobody particularly cares whether you are doing it as a hobby, that you are writing a family history, or that you want to leave with your children a knowledge of their heritage. You are gathering your genealogy -- compiling your family tree -- that is sufficient.

Unless you are writing to an intimate friend, don't write long, drawn-out letters -- at least not the first ones you write to anybody. Make them brief, but to the point. State briefly and clearly what you are looking for. Give enough information as to names, dates and places to put the recipient on the right track. One of the easiest ways to explain relationships is to send a short completed pedigree chart, showing the particular individuals involved in your inquiry.

You will save a lot of time and effort when writing for information if you use our Pedigree Chart No. P5. (See page 33) One side of that chart contains a short pedigree form and a printed letter asking for information. The pedigree form is a three generation chart. If you are asking for information on your paternal side, you need only to fill in the upper blanks of the chart; if on the maternal side, only the bottom section of the chart. The printed letter contains a blank space for you to fill in the name of the family you are seeking. The opposite side of the chart contains a four-generation pedigree chart which the recipient of your letter can fill in with the requested information. On this side also is a space for you to fill in the name and address of the person you are writing to. It is in such a position that the letter can be folded to fit a window envelope, thus avoiding the necessity of writing his name twice yet assuring you that his name will be on the sheet when it is returned.

Don't ask too many questions in your first letter. In subsequent letters, after relationship has been established, you may write more fully and more intimately. Then you may arrange your questions so that each one has a space following it for insertion of the answer. Always make it convenient for your correspondent to answer your questions with the least effort and in the shortest time possible. Courtesy demands that you enclose in your letter a stamped, self-addressed envelope unless you are writing to a public official or other person who is granted funds for such supplies. You should always offer to pay for any expense which might be incurred by the person gathering and compiling the information you want.

Be considerate in your requests. Don't ask for the sun, moon and the stars. Nobody will ever send them to you! One woman just starting out on her genealogical research wrote a man to send her "all the records you have on the So-and-So family." With a chuckle he tossed the letter in his yawning wastebasket, while he removed the stamp from the self-addressed envelope that had been enclosed with the letter. He deemed the request unworthy of any kind of a reply. For more than thirty years he had been gathering information on the So-and-So family until at that time his records were bulging with almost twenty thousand individual names and the necessary data pertaining to them.

Had the inquirer been conservative and asked for information about one particular individual, it would have been sent to her gladly.

Sometimes your letters will go unanswered though you have used all the proper methods and your requests have been within reason. It is our opinion that many of these letters are not answered because the person who received them just didn't have the information to help you. At least let us hope this is the case.

Someone has said that the best way to get people to treat you nicely is for you to treat them nicely. Some researchers have had success by sending a little gift in the letter, such as a handkerchief for a lady, etc. One man had some relatives in England who ignored his letters completely, but he sent them a few cans of peaches during the war years. They didn't ignore him any more.

CONTACT PERSONS OF SIMILAR NAMES

When searching for your family genealogy, you should never overlook any opportunity to contact people who may give you valuable information. In every large city in the nation are persons with the same surname as yours. Some of them may be distant relatives of yours. In starting your relative hunt, a short pleasant note identifying yourself by naming your father, grandfather, and great grandfather, generally will bring some answers in the self-addressed envelope you enclosed in your letter. If there is no relationship, they may refer you to someone elsewhere who may be a relative, or they may tell you of someone in their family who is compiling a family genealogy.

But how are you to find people of your surname? Nothing difficult about that at all. Most libraries have in their files city directories and telephone directories from various parts of the country. If they haven't, you may have access to telephone directories in your local telephone office. At the office of your Chamber of Commerce, you may find city directories from many other cities.

A MAGAZINE TO HELP YOU

THE GENEALOGICAL HELPER, a bi-monthly magazine founded in 1947, has aided thousands of people all over the world. It is dedicated to helping "more people find more genealogy." It is not confined to any particular section of the country but serves people in every state and many foreign countries. It is edited and published by the same concern publishing this book, The Everton Publishers Inc., P.O. Box 368, Logan, Utah 84321.

Four of the six bimonthly issues contain not fewer than forty-eight pages, each eight and one-half by eleven inches. The March and September issues contain approximately two hundred or more pages and are called The Annual Exchange Editions. Each issue contains articles on various phases of genealogy, reviews of new genealogical books, Genealogical Miscellany column, classified and display advertising. The January issue includes the Question Box and a list of all active Family Associations with their leaders. March isssue is the Semi-Annual Exchange Edition and contains the registrations of many enthusiastic genealogists. The registrations have a surname index in this issue. May edition features a special section on a certain country or state and also has the Question Box. July's special feature is a current listing of Genealogical Societies, Libraries and Professional Genealogists and also has the Question Box. The September magazine contains the Annual Exchange Edition and will be indexed similarly to the March issue. November's issue will contain the Question Box (free query section for subscribers) and a surname index of all advertisements and articles in the "Helper" for that year.

The first Annual Exchange Edition of "The Genealogical Helper" was published in 1950. Every year since then it has gained in popularity as thousands have found it pays to let the genealogical world know of their ancestor enigmas through its columns. Over the years there probably have been between thirty and forty thousand people who have "registered" their wants in the various Annual Exchange Editions. Many have sent unsolicited testimonials of how they have received the answers they wanted through someone reading their notice and volunteering the information. Other thousands have benefited by contacting those who have placed their names in the "Helper." If you are interested, send to The Everton Publishers, P.O. Box 368, Logan, Utah 84321, for the free catalogue which lists many other genealogical aids.

WHERE TO WRITE FOR GENEALOGY

A lot of personal and family information is available if one only knew where to go to find it. Although it takes a longer time, it is cheaper to write for that information unless you live in proximity to the old family home. Before addressing your envelopes, make out a list of the persons and organizations to which you intend to write. List the name and the complete address of each. After you are through with the list, place it in your genealogical file with a copy of your letter so you can find it anytime you desire to check it. When writing to strangers or organizations, it is always best to enclose a stamped self-addressed envelope for the expected reply. Don't be irritated if we remind you of that courtesy too often -- we believe it is for your best interests. The following list is only suggestive. You may think of many more.

Relatives, all kinds, everywhere.
Friends of the family, all dates.

Residents and former neighbors of the old home town.

Postmaster of the above, to locate relatives.

Names found in newspapers.

Names from directories.

City recorders, to locate records.

County judges, or county clerks, about marriage bonds or licenses.

Family genealogists on your surname.

Genealogists living near the old home town.

Genealogical book stores for family and county histories.

Genealogists who search census records.

National Archives and libraries for early census.

Quaker researchers.

Immigration Bureau for arrivals.

Persons of your surname.

Genealogical libraries.

Bureau of Vital Statistics, each state capitol.

Newspapers for classified advertisements and old obituary notices.

LDS Church Historian's Office, Salt Lake City, Utah.

Rectors of English parishes.

Genealogists searching Great Britain Census.

Dominion Archives for Canadian census. "Letters to the Editor" or forums of newspapers to locate unknown friends or relatives of the old home town.

WRITING TO PUBLIC OFFICERS

No uniform method of record keeping is used by town and county offices. Some have cemetery or burial records that began many years ago. Some have birth records. Others have printed records of births, marriages and deaths, as well as other valuable information about the early settlers of the community. In each case it would be well to write the city recorder and ask for the information you want. If he does not have the records you want, he will direct you where to write.

The same is true of the county records. Various counties have used different methods of record keeping. Many counties throughout the United States have printed county histories with a lot of genealogy. Some have good records of wills and deeds and civil court actions. From all of these a great deal of genealogical information can be culled. If you find they have wills or other records pertaining to your family, a photostat copy will cost very little. A letter to the county clerk or the clerk of the court will bring from him the information you desire. Also if you find a book with a page or two of data you would like to have for your own, photostats of these may be made.

Much more information on writing to public officials and others may be found in HANDBOOK FOR GENEALOGICAL CORRESPONDENCE and THE HANDY BOOK FOR GENEALOGISTS. Both may be purchased from The Everton Publishers. (See page 235).

USE LABOR SAVING DEVICES

Sometimes you have to write to many people to locate a lost relative. It takes a lot of time and effort to write the same kind of letter to fifty or a hundred persons. It will be easier on your nerves to have the letter mimeographed. If you have a typewriter you can cut the stencil yourself, thus cutting the cost materially. Almost every county seat or high school will have a typewriter service equipped with mimeograph material, and by using it you can cut the cost of your letters down to a few cents each. In some cases it may pay you to include a pedigree chart to give the recipient a better idea of your family connections. We again refer you to the P5 pedigree chart mentioned in the previous chapter -- it will save a lot of labor, will clearly state your wants and make it easy for your correspondents to answer. Possibly you can make up your own letter and chart to serve your purposes even better.

FAMILY GENEALOGISTS

There are no more willing cooperators in this work than the family genealogists. They are active in this pursuit for the same reason that you are. The easiest way to learn of them and their addresses is to secure a copy of one of the Annual Exchange Editions of THE GENEALOGICAL HELPER. Many libraries in the nation are subscribers to that magazine. If they are not, suggest to them to subscribe to it now, or you can send for a copy yourself. Remember, each January issue of the "Helper" has a list of family organizations.

You may greatly enrich your records by writing to all those persons listed who are compiling data on the families shown on your pedigree chart. This is especially true if their family and your family lived in the same state. Like you, those people are compiling their own family genealogy, and they have access to information not printed in any book.

HOME TOWN GENEALOGISTS

A genealogist living where your ancestors resided generally has access to records unknown to you. He is undoubtedly a member of a county historical society which has spent years in collecting data on the early inhabitants of the county. He has access to birth and marriage records, death and cemetery records.

Sometimes you may get a lot of information for nothing. However, you should remember that it takes a lot of time to search the records. If you get a letter telling you of available material but that it will cost you a certain amount of money for the time involved, accept the offer if you can afford to pay for it and it seems reasonable.

Most researchers occasionally find knotty problems which stump them. The quickest way to get a problem solved may be to engage the services of an expert. A professional genealogist who has spent years in research, who has searched for many family lines in many places and who is a specialist in the genealogy of one particular part of the country or of one special kind of records, often can solve a problem quickly because he knows just where and how to look. Each July issue of THE GENEALOGICAL HELPER has a list of professional genealogists. If you desire the services offered by them you should check their qualifications and fields of research in the latest issue.

Time has been a great aid to the researcher. What appeared as an insurmountable problem years ago can often be solved easily today. Thousands of old records hidden away in unknown places have been discovered, have been indexed and made easily available to the researcher. They have cleared up many problems that previously baffled the searcher. Every year sees hundreds of "lost" records coming to light.

WRITE TO GENEALOGICAL LIBRARIES

Good results have been obtained from

writing to genealogical libraries. The librarian knows what is in the library and with a minimum of effort can find the data wanted. If you send a stamped envelope you will receive a courteous reply in most cases. Past experience indicates most librarians will attempt to find the information you are seeking if it does not entail too much searching.

Information regarding residents of the county in which located is a specialty with most libraries. For that reason, it may be well to write the library in the state and county where your people lived. Many times the small local libraries have information not obtainable in the larger libraries. Again, the July issue of THE GENEALOGICAL HELPER may help you as it lists libraries and Genealogical Societies of each state.

When you write to a library do not send a list of names. Ask about the ancestry of just one man or a man and his wife. Make identification easy by giving names of persons desired and whatever identifying information you have about them.

PRINTED FAMILY HISTORIES

An easy way to seek genealogy is to find

the results of research done by others. A man sometimes spends a lifetime and a small fortune in searching for his family history and getting it printed in book form. When it is printed, one often can buy a copy of the book for five to ten dollars, even though thousands of dollars have been expended to get it printed. You may even be able to borrow it from the library. When you find a book, however, as mentioned before, be sure to verify every step you may find in it that pertains to your direct ancestors.

During the past fifty years or more thousands of people have become interested in genealogy. Doctors, lawyers, educators, workmen in various fields, housewives, and office workers -- in fact, people in all walks of life -- have suddenly become interested in searching for their ancestors. The desire to learn something about their progenitors seems to have struck them all at once. Enthusiastically they have searched among family relics, histories and official records. They have gathered information tirelessly for twenty or thirty years or more to satisfy the urge that has constantly been with them, spurring them on in their efforts to locate every source of information possible.

Many of them have expended many thousands of dollars to secure their records. Generally few of them become satisfied with their work until they have produced a printed volume for the safe-keeping of their laboriously compiled history.

With the invention of new printing methods, family records can now be produced to fit almost any purse; they can be mimeographed, lithographed or letterpress printed.

One of the neatest and most interesting family records we have seen was also the easiest understood. It was the work of an architect and was built around our Pedigree Chart No. P8 and Family Group Sheet No. F2. Each sheet was first typewritten. Interspersed among these sheets were plain bond sheets, S5, on which were typewritten family and personal histories about the individuals mentioned on the preceding charts. This matter was typewritten in two four-inch columns on each sheet. The families were arranged and mentioned in the following order: The author, his wife and their children, his parents and their children, his grandparents and their children, his great grandparents and their children, his great great grandparents and their children, etc. Picture pages were also included.

The wife's family can be included following the completion of the husband's family.

Some family histories begin with the oldest known progenitor and come down step by step to the present. In some cases each individual mentioned has been ingeniously numbered. For instance, if the first progenitor known is numbered 1, his first child, regardless of sex, becomes 11, the second 12, the third 13, etc. If someone is of the tenth or eleventh generation, the number may be one such as this: 1253-10-264, in which: No. 1 is the original ancestor thus far known; the figure 2 indicates the second child of No. 1; the figure 5 indicates the fifth child of the preceding No. 2; the figure 3 indicates the third child of the preceding No. 5; the number 10 indicates the tenth child of the preceding No. 3 (only numbers ten and above are hyphenated); the following No. 2 indicates the second child of the preceding No. 10 and so on. Only the direct descendants in the family are numbered. Wives and husbands of the direct descendants are mentioned only, not numbered. With this method, no two descendants of the same individual can have exactly the same number. Many other ways of numbering genealogical works have been devised. You may be able to figure out a system that will suit your particular record better than the above or any other used heretofore.

LIBRARY CATALOGUES

More and more libraries are printing catalogues of the books they have in their various departments. The names of family histories and their authors are always included. If such catalogues are not available it is sometimes possible to learn from the librarian of any of the libraries in or near the locality of your early families whether or not histories of those families are available. If a library refuses to let you borrow a book, you may be able to hire someone there to check the book for you to determine if any of your relatives are included. By getting the name and address of the publisher of the book you may be able to purchase a copy, or gain access to one.

It often costs less to buy a genealogical book than to hire someone to copy the information you need. It is always more satisfactory to own a book than to borrow it if it contains much information for you. Today there are more family histories than ever before. Because only a limited number of copies of such histories are printed, the cost is much higher than the popular novel which is printed by the tens or hundreds of thousands. A genealogical book that looks like a dollar book may sell for $5.00 or more. Still, if you can buy a book for $5.00 you cannot afford to pay for getting it copied.

If you live in or near a large city, it may pay you to spend several hours in a second-hand bookstore once in a while. Browse around and thumb through book after book to get the general idea of their contents. Sometimes you'll find something that is just exactly what you want. Do the same thing in libraries you visit.

BORROWING GENEALOGICAL BOOKS

One of the privileges that comes with joining certain genealogical societies is that of borrowing books from their libraries even if you live thousands of miles from them. The annual dues generally are around $15, besides which you must have to pay the postage both ways on the books you borrow. If you are interested, write to the particular society for information as to costs, etc. One of the foremost societies is the New England Historical Genealogical Society, 101 Newbury Street, Boston, Mass. 02116. Their dues entitle you to the magazine published quarterly. The society owns one of the largest genealogical libraries in the United States.

If you join certain patriotic societies, such as the Sons of the American Revolution or the Daughters of the American Revolution, you also may have access to information they have gathered over a hundred years or more.

Sometimes libraries in smaller cities are able to borrow books from the state library or other large institutions. Contact your librarian and ask for help to get what you would like to obtain.

RECORDS IN NATIONAL ARCHIVES

WAR RECORDS. Every state in the union which furnished soldiers for the Revolutionary War has histories containing the names of these men, and the branch of the service in which they were enlisted. In 1818 Congress passed an act establishing the first service pension law in the United States and provided pensions for all who had served at least nine months and were in indigent circumstances. In 1820 the War Department published the names of those who had applied for this pension. They were listed according to the states in which the enlistment was made. In 1955 the Genealogical Publishing Co., 521-23 St. Paul Place, Baltimore, Md. 21202, reprinted this valuable list containing more than 17,000 names. If one or more of your early American ancestors participated in the Revolutionary War and later received a pension, the names should be in that book. The names from each state are arranged in alphabetic order, making it easy to find the names in which you are interested. If the person did not apply for a pension you still may be able to find his name in one of the rosters published by the various states.

More often than not, the pension applications of soldiers contain valuable genealogical information. Sometimes it pays the researcher to obtain at a reasonable cost a photostat copy of the application. The pension records are in the National Archives in Washington, D.C. If you can't personally visit the Archives, it is necessary for you to employ a researcher to search the records for the needed information. Lists of researchers available for assignments in the National Archives and Library of Congress may be obtained on application to those agencies in Washington, D.C. The Historical Societies in the respective states oftentimes have valuable information about service men also.

WAR RECORDS HELP

Most libraries throughout the United States have on their shelves copies of state histories containing information about soldiers of the various wars of the United States and the earlier Colonial America. If your ancestors date to the earliest days of America they may have been participants in some of the following wars fought here: King William's War, 1690 to 1697, fought mainly in Canada; Queen Anne's War, 1702 to 1713, also fought in Canada; King George's War, 1744 to 1748, conducted on this side of the Atlantic mainly on the island of Cape Breton, between Nova Scotia and Newfoundland, where the French military post of Louisburg was captured by the

British in 1745, but returned to the French in 1748; French and Indian War, 1745 to 1763, involving Ohio and Quebec, through which England gained control of everything east of the Mississippi River; The Revolutionary War, 1775 to 1783, which brought about the founding of the United States of America; the War of 1812, declared by the United States against Great Britain, and fought in diverse places, north and south, and brought about no new borders; the Mexican War, 1846 to 1848, which gained us the territory now including several of our western states; the Civil War, 1861 to 1865, the conflict between the north and the south over slavery; the Spanish American War, April 1898 to August 1898, which added to our possession the Philippines, Puerto Rico and Cuba.

CENSUS RECORDS

A census, a count of all inhabitants, has been taken in most countries since the days of the Roman Empire. It was to comply with the practice that Mary and Joseph left their home in Nazareth to go to Bethlehem, to be counted among the descendants of David, at the time of the birth of Christ. Since then, enumeration has been practiced in all countries under various names. In Europe it is done under the auspices of the dominant church as well as by the respective governments.

Since 1790 the government of the United States has conducted a census every ten years. At first only the name of the head of the family was required with an indication of the number of persons in the family. Later, the numbers of persons within specific age groups were reported, and the census now lists the complete name of each person, address, age, occupation and other information. The 1790 census was taken in each of the seventeen states then existing. Since then each new state as it has been created has been included in the succeeding enumerations.

It must be remembered that no census ever taken is absolutely correct, either as to the information recorded or as to the completeness of listing of all persons living at that time. Enumerators have made many mistakes in writing the data required, and many people lived beyond the areas assigned to be counted or were accidently missed. Census records should be used mainly as guides for clues and not as absolute proof of any point.

The 1880 U.S. census is the latest made record available to the public. Some close relatives may receive information from later censuses by writing for an "Age Search Application" form from Personal Service Branch, Bureau of the Census, Pittsburg, Kansas 66762.

NATURALIZATION RECORDS

All foreign-born residents of the United States have had the opportunity to become citizens of this nation by observing certain stipulations, which have changed from time to time. A record of naturalizations has been kept since 1740. If the naturalization took place before 27 September 1906, the search for it should be conducted in the office of the respective county clerk; if after that date information may be obtained from the Commissioner of Immigration and Naturalization, Washington, D.C. 20536.

The naturalization record contains the following description of the holder: age, height, color, complexion, color of eyes, color of hair, and visible distinguishing marks; name, name of spouse and residence;

names, ages and places of residence of minor children; and the name of the country from which the holder came. Earlier naturalization certificates also gave the place and date of entry of holder to the United States, and may thus direct attention to passenger lists maintained in the National Archives.

PASSENGER LISTS

Among important books of the earliest arrivals of persons in America are:

Hotten, John Camden. THE ORIGINAL LIST OF PERSONS OF QUALITY WHO WENT FROM GREAT BRITAIN TO THE AMERICAN PLANTATIONS. Reprinted by The Genealogical Publishing Co., Baltimore, Maryland. (1968).

Strassburger, Ralph Beaver. PENNSYLVANIA GERMAN PIONEERS. Reprinted in 2 Vols. by Genealogical Publishing Company, Baltimore Maryland (1966).

Rupp, I. Daniel. THIRTY THOUSAND NAMES OF IMMIGRANTS. Reprinted by Genealogical Publishing Co., Baltimore, Maryland (1965).

Pope, Charles Henry. THE PIONEERS OF MASSACHUSETTS. Reprinted by Genealogical Publishing Company, Baltimore, Maryland (1965).

Evjen, John O. SCANDINAVIAN IMMIGRANTS IN NEW YORK, 1630-1674, with Apprendices on Settlements in Mexico and South America 1530 to 1640 and in Canada, 1619 to 1620. K.C. Holter Publishing Co., Minneapolis, Minn. (1916).

Pearson, Jonathan. FIRST SETTLERS OF SCHENECTADY, N.Y., 1662 to 1800. J. Munsell, 82 State Street, Albany, N.Y. 12207.

Coulter, E. Merton and Saye, Albert B. A LIST OF THE EARLY SETTLERS OF GEORGIA. University of Georgia Press, Athens, Georgia (1949).

Currer-Briggs, Noel. VIRGINIA SETTLERS AND ENGLISH ADVENTURES. (Three columes in one) Reprinted by Genealogical Publishing Company, Baltimore, Maryland (1970).

Farmer, John. A GENEALOGICAL REGISTER OF THE FIRST SETTLERS OF NEW ENGLAND. Reprinted with additions and corrections by Samuel G. Drake, Genealogical Publishing Company, Baltimore, Maryland (1969).

Drake, Samuel G. RESULT OF SOME RESEARCHES AMONG THE BRITISH ARCHIVES FOR INFORMATION RELATIVE TO THE FOUNDERS OF NEW ENGLAND. Reprinted by Genealogical Publishing Co., Baltimore, Maryland (1969).

Waters, Henry F. GENEALOGICAL GLEANINGS IN ENGLAND. Reprinted by Genealogical Publishing Co., Baltimore, Maryland (1969).

Transcripts made by the State Department. PASSENGERS WHO ARRIVED IN THE UNITED STATES SEPTEMBER 1821 - DECEMBER 1823. Magna Charta Book Co., Baltimore, Maryland (1969).

Kaminkow, Jack and Marion. A LIST OF EMIGRANTS FROM ENGLAND TO AMERICA 1719-1759. Magna Charta Book Co., Baltimore, Maryland (1964).

Jacobus, Donald Lines. INDEX TO GENEALOGICAL PERIODICALS. Reprinted by Genealogical Publishing Co., Baltimore,

Maryland (1969).

Swem, E.G. VIRGINIA HISTORICAL IN-
DEX 2 Vols. Reprinted in Northampton,
Mass.: Peter Smith (1964).

Lancour, Harold. A BIBLIOGRAPHY OF
SHIP PASSENGER LISTS 1538-1825. New
York Public Library, N.Y. (1963).

Banks, Charles Edward. THE PLANTERS
OF THE COMMONWEALTH. Genealogical
Publishing Co., Baltimore, Maryland (1967).

Noyes, Sybil; Libby, Charles Thornton;
and Davis, Walter Goodwin. GENEALOG-
ICAL DICTIONARY OF MAINE AND NEW
HAMPSHIRE. 5 Vols. Printed by Southworth
Press, Portland, Maine (1928-1938).

THE NEW ENGLAND HISTORICAL AND
GENEALOGICAL REGISTER. Published
since 1847 by New England Historic Genealogical Society, Boston, Massachusetts.

Bolton, Ethel. IMMIGRANTS TO NEW ENG-
LAND 1700-1775. Reprinted by Genealogical
Publishing Co., Baltimore, Maryland (1967).

The National Archives also have the passenger lists of vessels from foreign ports arriving in Baltimore, 1820 to 1919; Boston from 1883 to 1899; New Orleans from 1820 to 1897; and New York City from 1820 to 1919; lists of sailors on vessels of American Merchant Marine from 1916 to 1941, and lists of numerous persons formerly employed by various agencies of the American government.

LAND RECORDS

Of genealogical value equal to that of such statistical data, such as birth, marriage and death records, are the land records and wills. They often reveal relationships not otherwise recorded and usually are not difficult to obtain. You may have a photostatic copy at a reasonable cost from the clerk of the county in which your ancestors lived. To help find information you must give the time in which your ancestors lived in a locality and their full names.

To get similar information from Europe it is best to hire a professional genealogist in the particular country, or find some place where the microfilms of the records are available. One of the books which may

help you as you cross the Atlantic is
"American Origins" by L.G. Pine, pub-
lished by Doubleday and Co., Garden City,
N.Y. 11530.

THE HANDY BOOK FOR GENEALOGISTS

As you start to do research in specific
localities you want to know considerable
about that part of the country. It will be ad-
vantageous, for instance, to know about
migrations to and from that section -- you
will want to know about the formation of
the counties, where their records are kept,
who to write to, etc.

Much of this information is found in the
"Handy Book for Genealogists," published
by The Everton Publishers and probably
available through the merchants from whom
you purchased this book. It contains
maps of 50 states and many foreign countries
which show the boundaries of counties. It
tells when the counties were formed and the
parent county or territory from which it
was formed. It lists the county seats and
capitals where records of births, marriages
and deaths are kept, also to whom to write
to for certified copies of information recorded there. It tells when many of the

countries and counties started their records and the type of records available.

This type of information will give you inestimable help getting the data you need. You will be able to decide quickly where to go or to whom to write to get enlightenment on official records such as wills, deeds, court records, vital statistics, etc. Much other general information on the various states and European countries is given, such as population, migrations, libraries, genealogical societies, etc., making it one of the most popular genealogical books ever printed. Over 100,000 copies are now in use.

The introduction to THE HANDY BOOK FOR GENEALOGISTS, Sixth Edition has so many good pointers for genealogists, it is being reprinted here almost verbatim. Of course, you will have to consult the book itself to get the information you need but you will find most libraries have copies. If you do a lot of research you will undoubtedly want a copy of your own. The problems presented and their solutions are typical of thousands of enigmas you may find as you search for forebears. You should garner many ideas on how to overcome your research perplexities just from the introduction.

INTRODUCTION TO
THE HANDY BOOK FOR GENEALOGISTS
SIXTH EDITION

''As you start to gather information for your family tree you may find undoubtedly that your American ancestors migrated from place to place. It is a rare thing to find even two or three generations of a family at one location. If they were not in one of the mass movements from Europe to America or from the eastern seaboard on west, they were looking, nevertheless, for greener pastures and changed their abodes - sometimes so often it is extremely difficult to follow their trails.

''As they moved from one country, state or county to another they usually left records. You must find those records to verify births, deaths, marriages and many other facts regarding their lives and loves. You must follow their trails sometimes backward and forward. It is not unusual for genealogists to work on both ends of the trail, finally closing the gap, making a complete record of their movements and many other interesting facts about their lives.

''When you start your search for their records you may find some in one state and some in another. It is also possible you will find some of your progenitors living in one place for many years, yet their records are scattered in several counties. This may have been caused by their original counties being divided and subdivided again and again. How to search for these records at one time presented a great challenge, but ''The Handy Book for Genealogists'' gives answers to thousands of these questions quickly, easily.

''Many of the older genealogists have said they wished they could have had this aid when they started research. They had to dig facts regarding the dates of organization of counties and their parent counties from history books, county commission and legislature minutes books and many other kinds of archival material. By trial and error they found where records were kept, what they revealed, etc. These facts must be known in practically all cases before you can get information needed to establish your connections.

''Knowing what records are available and who to contact for extracts or copies also presents a tremendous problem as each country, state and county may have different record keeping systems. The county clerk may have the records you need in one county, the city clerk in another, the clerk of the court in another, and the state health department in another. With this book you can decide quickly where to write for records.

"To assist you in the use of information you have in this volume let us illustrate with some hypothetical cases:

1. STATE HISTORIES

"Tradition states one of your great grand parents was born in Missouri in 1811. You check the history of Missouri in "The Handy Book" and find it did not become a territory until 1812 - that from 1805 to 1812 it was part of Louisiana Territory. Therefore, it would be unlikely Missouri would have a record about him or his parents in 1811. If you wanted to start a search, the place to look would be in Louisiana records. Of course, you might find he was not born in Missouri or in 1811 - that his parents brought him from another state as a babe or any one of a dozen other possibilities. One certain thing you would know is that the Territory of Missouri was not created until 1812, one year

after his traditional birth, and prior to that
time the section belonged to the Territory of
Louisiana.

2. COUNTY HISTORIES

"Suppose that you had a progenitor who
was one of the first settlers at Key West,
Florida. He took his family there in 1822 but
died in 1823 leaving his wife and children. You
want to know if there is a will, record of real
estate, or any other contemporary record
about him in the county records. You find that
Key West is the county seat of Monroe
County, but none of their records help you.
You wonder if something might be found
in adjoining counties but your search is fruit-
less in six or eight neighboring counties.
Finally you learn about the "Handy Book for
Genealogists," you turn to the Florida section and find Monroe County was formed in
1824 from St. John County, one year after the
death of your forefather. A further check reveals that St. Augustine is the county seat of
St. John County and it is almost on the other
side of the state, over 375 miles from
Key West. You go to the records at St. Augustine and find just what you want there.

"Next you search for the records of a fore-bear who lived and died in Ford County, Illinois. He was 75 years old at his death in 1869 - making his birthdate ca. 1794. You have reason to believe he was born at or near his place of death and would like to know everything possible about him from the county records. You check Ford County on page 58 of "The Handy Book" and find it was formed in 1859 from Clark County. Going back, you find that Clark was formed in 1819 from Crawford which was formed from Edwards in 1816. In turn, Edwards was formed in 1814 from Madison and Gallatin, they being formed in 1812, St. Clair, which was formed from the N. W. Territory in 1790, was the parent county of Madison. Randolph, formed from St. Clair and the N.W. Territory in 1795, was the parent county of Gallatin.

"You must search the records of six or seven counties to be sure you have all that can be found about a man who supposedly lived all his life within the confines of one county: Ford 1869-1859; Clark 1859-1819; Crawford 1819-1816; Edwards 1816-1814. Then Madison 1814-1812; St. Clair 1812-1794 or Gallatin 1814-1812; Randolph 1812-1794. It might pay to do further investigating to establish whether your research should go to Madison or Gallatin Counties. It would undoubtedly not be both.

3. LIBRARIES

"One of your ancestors came from Connecticut. What library might have records on his life? You check the list of libraries on page 28 and find quite a number you can write to for information. You also find several books listed which could be extremely helpful in your progenitor search.

4. MAPS

As you search in many U.S. counties you will find their records do not start until several years after the formation date found in the "Handy Book." This situation arose undoubtedly because the residents failed to take advantage of the enabling act. It is possible people were living there or legislature would not have acted. You will find it easy to locate your county and all surrounding counties from maps in the "Handy Book" and it might be well to check with neighboring county clerks to ascertain if they have some record of your ancestor. Occasionally persons would travel to one of the nearby counties for a marriage or other important business if it could not be taken care of in their own county.

"The maps of all the states show the adjoining counties in neighboring states. Thus you can follow migrations with much greater ease than heretofore.

"You follow the trail of one of your ancestors in his westward trek through Virginia. It starts at James City with one, two, or three stops in each of the following counties: Henrico, Buckingham, Roanoke and Scott. Here you loose the trail. You have reason to believe he moved across the line to Tennessee. You locate Scott County on the map and you find bordering on the south the Tennessee counties of Hancock, Hawkins and Sullivan - the three counties you will have to search to pick up the trail again.

5. COUNTY RECORDS

"A questionnaire was sent to every county clerk or clerk of court in the U.S. asking for information about the records in their custody. About 90% of them returned the questionnaire. Many gave information which should be helpful in searching county records. This information is included in this edition with the other county data. For instance you turn to Arkansas on page 12 and find that Arkansas County is the first county listed. Under this county you find: (Co Clk has

pro rec from 1809, m rec from 1838; Clk Cir
Ct has div & civ ct rec from 1803, War ser
discharge from 1917.) Interpreted this says:
County Clerk has probate records from 1809,
marriage records from 1838; Clerk Circuit
Court has divorce and civil court records
from 1803 and War service discharges from
1917.

6. GENEALOGISTS' CHECK LIST OF HISTORICAL RECORDS SURVEY.

"Surveys of public record archives were
conducted in most states during 1936 to 1943
by the Works Progress Administration
(WPA), a government agency. For example,
inventories were made of federal archives
in all the states, some county and municipal
archives, transcripts of some public archives, directories of church archives and
religious publications, guides to public vital
statistics records and depositories of manuscript collections, check lists of American
imprints, and various other surveys and list-
ings of records and archives of interest
to different types of researchers.

"A great many of the records, as you will
note, are vital to genealogical research, but
very few of the WPA publications give full

transcripts; they only name the records available in the respective archives. Quite often they tell the condition of the records, where they are stored, when the survey was made, and dates of commencement and conclusion of the records. The records themselves must be examined to gain the information.

"However, you may save much time in your data search by first consulting the check list, and then the survey, inventory or transcript to find out the existence of buried or piled up records in some county courthouse basement or attic, which may give contemporary evidence regarding the life of your ancestor.

"Of course, only a small portion of all available records and archives were surveyed, but those that were completed are a great help in locating records for research, finding what may be available, what the records contain, etc.

"Many times one will find unusual and extremely valuable records for genealogical research in county or other archives which are not common. A search should be made in each place to see if such records as naturalization papers, apprenticeship records,

special tax assessments, and many other
out-of-the-ordinary records are available,
as well as the usual wills, deeds, court and
vital records.

"From the Genealogists Check List of the
Historical Records Survey you can determine quickly if a survey was made by the
WPA. You should consult the survey to
ascertain what records are available in that
archive -- the usual and the unusual. You will
know then what to look for if you can visit the
place personally or what to write for if you
can't.

"A check list of these publications was
published by the WPA according to the type of
publication. Sometimes it takes a lot of
searching to find all records which might be
listed of one state or locality. Many publications are of little or no value to genealogists
since they pertain to such things as reports
and records of the Treasury Department and
other federal agencies none of which have any
personal records. They are of no value to the
genealogist.

"At the suggestion of Meredith B. Colket,
Jr., for many years director of the Institute
for Genealogical Research, sponsored by the

American University and the National Archives, George B. Everton, Sr., of The Everton Publishers undertook the assignment of making a rearranged check list of these WPA publications. Almost 2,000 books were examined and evaluated as to their genealogical value. The ones of no value to genealogists were eliminated from the list. The list was rearranged according to states, putting all publications of a state together. Thus, if you are searching for records of Missouri you can now find them all grouped together, making it possible to determine quickly if the records of any particular county, city, church or federal agency in Missouri was surveyed for records of genealogical nature. If so, then you should try to get the publication to determine if any records might be available which would assist you.

"Of course, as with most records, you will find some of the listed publications greater value than others. For instance, Ship Registers and Enrollments have only slight value to genealogists. Nevertheless, the names of the owners and captains of these ships are easy to check in the good indices and at times this may prove to be the only record you can find of these people. You may also find clues as to where other records may be found.

Don't be discouraged if some of the publications don't produce the information you need. Persistence is a virtue no genealogist can afford to overlook.

"Every state or region had a designated depository of unpublished material which may have many of the publications. An exchange was made at the time of printing whereby copies were supposed to be sent to each region or state depository. The depositories of unpublished materials -- which was in preparation for publication at the time the project was abandoned - are listed in the rearranged check list. Many libraries also have fair collections of the WPA Historical Records Survey Publications. At one time the Library of Congress acted as an exchange station, distributing surplus copies to other libraries and depositories. The staff of the National Archives Library, Washington, D.C. 20025, have endeavored to gather a complete set, but still lack some numbers. They have a few surplus copies they would be happy to exchange with other libraries or depositories, especially if they could fill in the ones they lack.

"You may find a copy of the publication you need close by; or you may have to do some searching. Check with your local library first and extend your search from there. If you can locate publications pertinent to the area and time of your ancestor you may save many hours of tedious labor, as they will show you quickly what records are available in each archive where surveys were made.''

EARLY SPELLING OF NAMES

Every surname may be spelled in several ways. The researcher should try to know all of them. You may be proud of your family name -- justly so -- but do not imagine it has always been spelled as it is now.

As a warning, researchers should weigh carefully the spelling of early family names, let us recall the familiar Kress name has been written in twenty-one different ways by priests and recorders of Europe namely: Krehs, Kresz, Kresze, Kreshe, Kresse, Kresso, Crezzo, Creso, Cresso, Chresos, Chrehse, Cresse, Chreshe, Crese, Cresze, Cres, Cras, Cresen, Creseno and Cresonis.

What is the reason for so many different spellings of names? Not so very long ago few people could read and fewer could write. The spelling of a family name was not of particular interest to members of the family. The minister or lawyer or landlord or county clerk spelled the names that came to them in their line of duty as they sounded to them. Any way they were spelled drew no comment from the family members. It is not particularly strange that each one who wrote the name may have spelled it in a new way, a different way. The same name may be spelled one way in the church record, another way in a deed, a third way in a will and a fourth way in the cemetery record, etc.

Whatever names you are interested in, try to find out the many different ways they may be spelled. When you come across the different varieties in your research, don't toss any of them aside, but take note of them and keep them in your record. They may come in handy sometime. If you pass up any of the different varieties of spelling, you may have to retrace your steps later and pick them up.

WHENCE CAME SURNAMES

Strange as it may seem, surnames have not always been used to designate a particular family. Early Bible characters, for instance, had only one name, such as Seth, Noah, Abraham. It was not until the days of Moses, when the population had grown into millions, that it became necessary to distinguish individuals having the same given name. There was Korah, the son of Izhar, the son of Kohath, the son of Levi, recognizing four generations; there was Joshua the son of Nun; Jair the son of Manasseh. By the time of Christ, the custom of adding surnames had become common. We read of Simon BarJona. The word Bar meaning son, it would be Simon son of Jona, or to put the later Scandinavian touch to it, Simon Jonasson. About that time are also noted the locality and the character descriptive names, such as Simon of Cyrene, and Simon the Zealot.

In the Roman heyday we find the aristocratic families rather generous with their use of names, giving each person a Christian name, a clan name and a family name. Thus we meet Caius Julius Caesar, Marcus Tullius Cicero, Publius Vergilius Maro, and many other similar three-part names.

With the fall of the Roman culture and the ascendency of barbarianism names went back to the simple standard.

According to Prof. Osborne J.P. Widtsoe, on whose "An Introduction to the Study of English Surnames" these paragraphs are based, surnames have originated in the following ways; patronymic, derived from the father's name; local, from the designation of the property owned, or from some local peculiarity of the home; occupational, from trades or occupations followed; official, from some rank or office held; or nicknames.

France adopted surnames about 1000 A.D.; England, at least among the leading families, about the time of William the Conquerer. The Domesday Book reveals the early use of surnames. Before that time it was common to speak of a man as the son of his father. In Wales was used the word ap, meaning son of, as ap Rice, ap Evan, etc. When ap came before a vowel sound, the two words were combined, resulting in a new name, as Pugh from Ap-Hugh, Price from Ap-Rice, Bowen from Ap-Owen, Pritchard from Ap-Richard, Powell from Ap-Howell, etc.

Similarly surnames were derived from the French prefix fitz, coming from the Latin filius meaning son, such as Fitzsimon, Fitzgerald, Fitzpatrick, etc., or from the Gallic mac, also meaning son, resulting in McFarland, Mac Donald, McMaster, etc.

The Norman-French diminutives <u>ot</u> and <u>et</u> have formed many surnames, such as Emmett from little Emma, Eliot from little Elias, Marriot from little Mary, Wilmot from little William; also the diminutives on and en have formed Alison from the son of little Alice; Huggins, the son of little Hugh, Robinson, the son of little Robert.

More names have been derived from localities than anything else. John of Gaunt (Ghent) became John a Gaunt, and then John Gaunt; or Henry of Hull became Henry a Hull and then Henry Hull; Jack of London became Jack a London and finally Jack London; Richard of Lancaster, Richard a Lancaster, Richard Lancaster.

Contraction of words has created these cycles in names: John at the Brook, John atte Brook, John at Brook, John a Brook, John Brook. When studying the old original records, it is well to remember that the name will no doubt appear in one or the other of these designations. One who lived near some oak trees first became atte Oaks, n Oaks, Noakes or Nokes. It is easy to see the derivation of Bywater, Bywood, By-the-way, Bygates, Byatts, or Fieldman, Fielding, Bridgeman, Beecher, Beechman, Churcher,

Churchman, Kirkman, Wood, Atwood, Openshaw (an open small woody covert), Ogden, (hog den), Swinden, Graves, Cluff, Knowles (tree-less gently-rising grassy slopes). Tillers of the soil have been named Farmer, Plowman, Gardiner, Tillman, Mower, Cropper, Dyker, Dykeman, Drayner, Marler, Akerman, Beeman, Beaman, Woodman, Hewer, Herd, Hurd, Heard, Stotherd, Stoddard, Shepherd, Goddard, (goat herd) Swinart, Hoggart, Soward, Thatcher, Hillyer (from hillier, a roofer), Tyler, Slater, Slatter, Cotter, Cotterel, Cotterell, Miller, Milne, Milner, Mills, Smith, Wright, Cart-Wright, Wagoner, Driver, Chapman, Chipman, (the buyer), Packman, Paxman, Weaver, Wolman, Woolsey, Webster, (female weaver), Dyer, Brewer, Brewster, Tapper, Tapster, Potter, Crocker, Chandler (candle-maker), Forester, Forster, Foster, Woodruff, (guard of the woods), etc.

CLUES IN NAMES

Unusual Christian names often furnish a clue to which family a group may belong. For instance, one of the early Hales was named Jonathan. This Jonathan has thousands of descendants now, scattered far and wide. Wherever you find descendants of this

Jonathan you are apt to find a Jonathan Hale in the proximity. In unrelated Hales families this is more than likely not the case. There are some names, such as John, Thomas, James, etc., that are common in almost all families and one could not get a reliable clue from such. Of course, care must be exercised even with the most unusual names as there is no proof unless corroborative evidence is found.

When you find a given or middle name that sounds like a surname, it may be the surname of the individual's mother or grandmother. This clue is worth investigating.

A book that may help you more in the study of surnames is "Your Book of Surnames" by Pennethorne Hughes, Published by Faber & Faber, 24 Russell Sq., London, 1967.

APPROXIMATING DATES

Quite often you may find among your relatives one whose birthdate is not available. To place such a one in relation to other names on your chart, you may if you desire, use an approximate date of birth. It is always well to take into consideration the marriage date of the parents, if that is available, and the birthdates of other children in the family.

Statistics have been gathered from thousands of families in various countries and the following figures represent the average of the whole group. The average age of fathers at the birth of the first child is 26 years and of mothers it is 22 years. If you have the birthdate of only one child and do not know which child it is, first or a later one, the average age of the father will be 32 years and of the mother 28 years. Remember that these figures are averages only and will be wrong more often than right. Count the approximate age at marriage at 25 years for the man and 21 years for the woman. If you have the death date you are fortunate but you cannot approximate the birthdate from that unless the age at death is given. Approximate dates should be marked "about" and it is well to indicate how the approximation was arrived at.

RELATIONSHIP CHART

B = Brother
    or Sister
C = Cousin
CP = Common Progenitor
GGN = Great Grandnephew
    or Great Grandniece
GGS = Great Grandson
    or Great Granddaughter

GS = Grandson or
    Granddaughter
N = Nephew or Niece
R = Times removed
S = Son or Daughter

III
Relationships

If you have difficulties in figuring relationships on your lineal or collateral lines, close or distant, you will find the chart on page 138 a help. This chart, prepared especially for this publication, shows the relationship of descendants to a progenitor, also the relationship between the progenitor's descendants in any combination of degrees from him down to and including the tenth generation. Though there have been other systems of figuring relationships this is the most universal, being used in all courts of law and by major genealogical societies.

HOW TO USE RELATIONSHIP CHART

Note that the two upper columns are outlined in heavy lines. These are the common progenitor and his descendants. "CP" stands for common progenitor, the one who is the head of the two lines of descendants. "S" is his son or daughter as the case may be; "GS" his grandson or granddaughter; "GGS" his great grandson or great granddaughter; "2GGS" his second great grandson or second great granddaughter, and so on down to his eighth great grandson or granddaughter.

All the diamonds inside the heavy lines show relationship among his descendants. By following columns "1" from both sides of the chart we find they cross on the "B" diamond, showing that the sons of the common progenitor are brothers. By following columns "2" to the center we find they cross at the "1C" diamond, indicating that grandsons of the common progenitor are first cousins to each other. And so on down: great grandsons are second cousins; second great grandsons are third cousins; third great grandsons are fourth cousins, etc.

To this point few people have trouble in figuring relationships, but when they start to figure the "cousinship" and "times removed" they may have difficulty. With this chart one should find no trouble with any combination up to the tenth generation, and by following the pattern set by this chart he can go as many generations as he desires. Suppose that you want to figure your relationship to a distant cousin. You are eight generations removed from the common progenitor, or his sixth great grandson. Your "distant cousin" is six generations removed or his fourth great grandson on another line. To figure your exact relationship simply follow columns "8" on the one side and "6" on the other to where they cross and you find "5C 2R" indicating you are fifth cousins twice removed.

If you want to find your relationship to the son of your fifth great grandfather, follow columns "1" and "7" which show you are his fourth great grandnephew (4 GGN). Likewise, you are a first cousin six times removed (1C 6R) to the grandson of your sixth great grandfather.

Additional aids to understanding are the following:

The parents of your father or mother are your grandfather and grandmother and you are a grandson to them. (GS)

The parents of your grandfather or grandmother are your great grandparents and you are a great grandson to them. (GGS)

The parents of your great grandmother or great grandfather are your second great grandparents and you are a second great grandson to them, etc., (2GGS)

The children of your brothers and sisters are your nephews and nieces (N) and you are uncle or aunt to them.

The children of your nieces and nephews are your grandnieces or grandnephews (GN) and you are granduncle to them.

The children of your grandnephews and grandnieces are your great grandnephews or great grandnieces (GGN) and you are great granduncle to them.

Your father's brother or sister is your uncle or aunt and you are a nephew or niece to them. (N)

The children of your uncle or aunt are your first cousins and you are also their first cousin. (1C)

The children of your first cousins are first cousins once removed to you and you are the same to him or her. (1C 1R)

The son of your third great grandfather is your second great granduncle and you are a second great grandnephew or niece to him. (2GGN)

The children of your second cousins are your second cousins once removed and you are the same to them. (2C 1R)

The grandchildren of your second cousins are your second cousins twice removed and you are the same to them. (2C 2R)

A simple formula for figuring cousin relationships is this: Call the common ancestor "O" and count down to the subjects, subtract one from the smaller of the two figures - this is the cousin relationship. Then subtract the smaller number from the larger and this gives you the times removed. Example: one subject is seven steps down from the common ancestor, the other is four steps down - one from four is three, so the cousinship is third cousins, and four from seven is three (three times removed) making them third cousins three times removed (3C 3 R).

Another example:
Subject No. 1 is 9 steps down from the common ancestor.
Subject No. 2 is 6 steps down from the common ancestor.

6 - 1   5th cousin. 9 - 6   3 times removed.
So they are fifth cousins three times removed. (5C 3R).

Of course, if the steps down from the common ancestor are the same you simply subtract 1 from the number and it gives you
their cousinship and there are no times removed to be figured. Remember also that
the common ancestor is never counted when
figuring the steps down to the subject, just
as it appears on the chart on page 138.

NOTES

IV

Dictionary Of Genealogical Words, Terms And Abbreviations

This dictionary of genealogical terms and abbreviations is the largest ever presented to aid the novice or professional genealogist. It includes Latin, law, general words and phrases, abbreviations and hundreds of words from the languages of most of the European countries, all arranged in alphabetical order for ease of use. The inclusion of the many foreign words with the English is an innovation for this type of publication, but it should be much easier for you to find meanings with this arrangement, especially when foreign words are interspersed with English, as is sometimes the case.

References are made in the case of some terms as to where additional information may be found. A system has been devised to indicate which abbreviations are recognized and those not officially approved at this time.

An asterisk (*) proceeding a word indicates that word is not approved officially at this time. Where there is no asterisk, the word may or may not be approved. Many abbreviations not approved officially are in general use today by genealogists and may some day receive recognition. Others are abbreviations of the past -- which at times give the researcher considerable trouble because of their obscure meanings. Latin terms and abbreviations are included because Latin was the dominant language of schools, courts and churches during olden times and its influence is still felt in many records of modern times.

In the case of some words, only those meanings pertaining to genealogy are listed. No attempt has been made to segregate the meanings as to whether the word used in that sense would be a noun, verb, verb transitive or intransitive, adjective, adverb, etc. In some cases only the old or obscure meanings are given.

The following dictionaries were used in the compilation: "Webster's New International Dictionary", Second Edition, Unabridged, G. C. Merriam Co., 1949; "The American College Dictionary", Random House, 1951; "Handy Dictionary of the Latin and English Languages", David McKay Co., Philadelphia, 1948; "Cassell's Latin Dictionary", Funk and Wagnalls Co., N. Y. 1953 printing. The books listed under "Explanation of Terms and Symbols" were also used as were many others.

Your comments, suggestions and corrections will be welcomed for future editions.

EXPLANATION OF TERMS AND SYMBOLS

* - the asterisk indicates an abbreviation not recognized in Webster's New International Dictionary, Second Edition, G. C. Merriam Co., 1949. Examples: 1. adm.; *admin.; admr.; admstr., indicates all except "admin." are recognized as proper abbreviations of "administrator". 2. in the case of the abbreviation "an.", you will

find listed *annus; anno. This indicates
that "an." is recognized for anno but not
for annus. 3. k. *killed; king., indicates
that "k." is a proper abbreviation for king
and not killed. Nevertheless, you will find
in some of the old records that "k" is used
for killed. It may be used for other words
as well, as it would be almost impossible
to gather all abbreviations that have ever
been used in genealogical records -- attempt has been made only to gather and list
the more common ones. In the abbreviations of countries, states, cities, etc.,
no attempt has been made to distinguish
those recognized and not recognized.

ABC - "The ABC's of American Genealog-
    ical Research", by E. Kay Kirkham, pub-
    lished by Deseret Book Co., 1955.

(Aus) - Austria.
(Be) - Belgium.
(Can) - Canada.
(D) - Danish or Denmark.
(Du) - Dutch or Netherlands.
(E) - English or England.
(Fi) - Finnish or Finland.
(Fr) - French or France.
(G) - German or Germany.

GGR – "A Guide for Genealogical Research", by Archibald F. Bennett, published by Genealogical Society of the Church of Jesus Christ of Latter-day Saints, 1951.

1953 HB – "The 1953 Handy Book for Genealogists", by George B. Everton and Gunnar Rasmuson, published by the Everton Publishers, 1953.

(Ic) – Icelandic or Iceland.

(Ire) – Irish or Ireland.

(It) – Italian or Italy.

(L) – a Latin word or phrase.

(Ne) – Netherlands.

(No) – Norwegian or Norway.

p. – page. pp. – pages.

(q.v.) – the Latin abbreviation for "quode vide", meaning "which see".

(qq.v.) – the Latin plural of "which see". In other words when you find (q.v.) following a word, if you will turn to that word you will find additional information on the subject; (qq.v.) means to look up the words preceeding.

(Sc) – Scottish or Scotland.

(Sp) – Spanish or Spain.

SR – "Search and Research", by Noel C. Stevenson, copyright 1951 by Forrest Cool.

(SW) – Swedish or Sweden.

SYA - "Searching for Your Ancestors," by Gilbert Harry Doane, published by University of Minnesota, second printing, 1952.

(Sz) - Swiss or Switzerland.

(W) - Welch or Wales.

WMIA - "Ways and Means of Identifying Ancestors", by Evan L. Reed, published by Ancestral Publishing & Supply Co., 1947.

A

a. – *administration; annus (qq.v.); about; age; acre, acres.

A. Agder. (No) – Aust Agder.

aar (D) (No) – year.

ab. – *abbey (q.v.); about.

ab.(W) – son.

A. Bard. (Ic) – Auster-Barda strandarsysla.

abavus (L) – second great grandfather; ancestor.

abbey – a monastery ruled by an abbot or a convent ruled by an abbess. Abbr. – *ab., abb.

abbr.; abbrev. –abbreviated; abbreviation.

abjure – to renounce upon oath; to forswear; disavow. To abjure the realm was to swear, or take oath, to leave the country and never to return without leave of the king.

abjurer – one who abjures (q.v.).

abortivus (L) – stillborn.

Abp. – Archbishop.

abruptio (L) – breaking off; divorce.

*abs. abstr – abstract (q.v.)

abstract –a summary of the important points of a book or manuscript.

Abstract Books – books which list individual entries chronologically by district land office. (ABC p. 76).

abstract of title – a summary of the history of the title to land, showing liabilities and charges subject to the same.

abstract of will – a summary or an epitome of the will. In the genealogical sense an abstract of a will gives only the parts of the will which help in determining relationships, locations, etc.

abt. – *about.

Abu; Abou – literally, father; the first element in many Arabic proper names. Sometimes abbreviated to Bu.

abuela (Sp) – grandmother.

abuelo (Sp) – grandfather.

A.C. Ante Christum (L) – before Christ.

Acadia – the original name of Nova Scotia.

acc. – according (to); account; accompanied.

ach (W) – pedigree.

achievement – (Her.) an escutcheon with its helm, crest, mantle, supporters and motto.

achter-Kleindochter (Du) – great-granddaughter.

achter-kleinzoon (Du) – great-grandson.

ackd. – acknowledged.

ad. – addatur (q.v.).

AD. – *archdeaconry (q.v.).

A.D. - Anno Domini (q.v.).

a.d. - ante diem (q.v.).

adcon. - *archdeacon; *archdeaconry (qq.v.).

add. - addatur; adde (qq.v.).

addatur (L) - let there be added; add. Abbr. - ad.; add.

adde (L) - add. Abbr. - add.

adj. - *adjoining; adjourned

adlig (G) - noble.

ad loc. - ad locum (q.v.).

ad locum (L) - to or at the place. Abbr. - ad loc.

adm.; admin. - administrator (q.v.); administrative.

administration - the settling of an estate by one appointed by the proper court. Abbr. -*a.;*adm.; *adom.

administrator - the person appointed by court to settle an estate, either of one who is alive and proved incompetent, or an intestate (q.v.). He differs from an executor as he is appointed by the court, whereas the executor is appointed by the deceased and approved by the court. Should an executor by proved incompetent or otherwise unable to serve, the court may appoint an administrator in his place. Abbr. - adm.; *admin.; admr.;

adms.; admstr.

admr. - administrator (q.v.).

adom. -*administration (q.v.).

adopt - to take voluntarily a child of other parents to be in the place of, or as one's own child.

adoption - the act of adopting.

ad patres (L) - gathered to his father's; dead.

a.d.s. - autographed document signed.

ae.; aet. - aetatis (q.v.).

Aegidius (L) - Giles.

Aelizia (L) - Alice.

äeltester, aelteste (G) - oldest, eldest, Elder.

aetas (L) - life-time; age; generation.

aetat. - aetatis (q.v.).

aetatis (L) - of age. Abbr.- ae.; aet.; aetat.

aetatula (L) - very tender childhood.

affidavit - a sworn statement in writing, sworn to before proper authority. Abbr. - afft.

affinity - relationship by marriage between a husband and his wife's blood relations. Or between a wife and her husbands blood relations; in-law relationship.

afft. - affidavit (q.v.).

afsd. - *aforesaid.

aft. - *after; afternoon.

âge (Fr) - age.

agée (Fr) - aged.

agnates - a kinsman whose connection is traceable exclusively through males; any male relative by the father's side.

A.H. - Anno Hegirae, first year of Moslem era (A. D. 622).

A.H. - Anno Hebraico (q.v.).

ahne (G) - ancestor.

ahnentafel (G) - pedigree; a table of ancestors.

A.Hun. (Ic) - Austur-Hun-avatnssysla.

äidinsetä (Fi) - granduncle

äidinäiti (Fi) - grandaunt

ail hendaid (W) - 2nd great grandfather.

âine, âinée (Fr) - eldest.

äiti (Fi) - mother.

Akerhs. (No) - Akershus.

Ala. - Alabama.

Alanus (L) - Alan.

Alberedus; Aluredus (L) - Alfred.

alder (D) (No) - age.

älder (Sw) - age.

äldst, älst (Sw) - eldest.

aldste (D) - eldest.

Alesia, Aleysia (L) - Alice.

alias - another name; an assumed name.

Alienora (L) - Eleanor.

alien - a foreigner.

alienus (L)-another's; foreign; contrary; averse; hostile; insane; dis-

tracted.

alius (L) - another; other.

alleg. - *allegiance (q.v.).

allegation - application for license to marry.

allegiance - the relation of a feudal vassal, or leige man to his superior, or liege lord (qq.v.); the tie or obligation of a subject to his sovereign or government. Abbr. - *alleg.

Aloysius (L) - Lewis.

Alpes-Marit. (Fr) - Alpes-Maritimes.

als. - alias.

alt (G) - old.

alta. - Alberta.

alter (G) - age.

alumnus (L) - foster son.

Älvsbg. (Sw) - Älvsborg.

Amabilia (L) - Mabel.

amateur genealogist - one who cultivates the science or study of genealogy as an avocation for personal pleasure or gratification, without thought of monetary reward; not a professional. The matter of skill or ability has no weight, necessarily, in determining amateur or professional standing.

Ambrosius (L) - Ambrose.

Amia (L) - Amy.

amicus (L) - friend, ally, lover; patron; counsellor

amita (L) - father's sister

(aunt).

amita magna (L) – grandfather's sister; grandaunt.

amt (D) – county.

amt (No) – older name for county.

an. – *annus; anno (qq.v.).

Anabilia (L) – Annabel.

anc. – *ancestor.

ancêtres (Fr) – ancestors.

ancestor – one from whom a person is descended; any person of lineal or collateral relationship from whom property has been derived by descent. (An "X" is used in front of a name of a child on some family group sheets to designate one's ancestor).

ancestress – a woman ancestor.

anciano (Sp) – aged.

ancient district (Sc) – area larger than a county, as Galloway (included the countries of Wigton, Kirkudbright and southern parishes of Ayrshire), or Angus (included Forfarshire and part of Perthshire).

An. Do. – *Anno Domini (q. v.).

Andreas (L) – Andrew.

Anetavle (D) – pedigree.

anghyfreithlon (W) – illegitimate.

Angl. – Anglican, Anglicized.

Angl. (W) – Anglesey.

Anicetis Civitas (L) – In Dorsetshire.

änka (Sw) – widow.

änkeman (Sw) – widower.

änkling (Sw) – widower.

anmhriod (W) – unmarried.

Anna (L) – Anne.

année (Fr) – year.

anni (L) – years.

anno (It) – year.

anno (L) – in the year. Abbr. – an.

Anno Domini (L) – in the (specified) year of the Christian Era. Abbr. – A.D.; An. Do.; *Anno. Dom.

Anno Hebraico (L) – in the (specified) Hebrew year. (Add 3760 to the Christian year). Abbr. – A.H.

Anno Hegirae–first year of Moslem era (A.D. 622) Abbr. – A.H.

annor (L) – see annus.

Anno Regina Regis or Reginae (L) – in the year of the King's or Queen's reign. Abbr. – A.R.R.

anno regni (L) – in the year of the reign. Abbr. –a.r.

annosus (L) – aged, old.

annos vixit (L) – he lived (so many) years. Abbr. – a.v.

annus (L) – year; season; year's produce; age.

Abbr. - a.; *an.; *ano.; (also anno, annor).

ano; - *another; *annus (q. v.).

año (Sp) - year.

Ano. Dom. - *Anno Domini (q. v.).

anonyma (L) - stillborn daughter.

anonymus (L) - stillborn son.

antavla (Sw) - pedigree.

ante (L) - before.

antecedent - one's ancestry, past life, education, etc.

ante diem (L) - before the day. Abbr. - a.d.

ante-hac (L) - before this time; earlier.

antenato (It) - ancestor.

antenupital contract - a contract made before marriage, usually made in contemplation of marriage, esp. between the parties as to their property rights.

antepasados (Sp) - ancestors.

Anthonius (L) - Anthony.

Antona Borealis (L) - Northampton.

Antwerp. (Bel) - Antwerpen.

anus (L) - old woman.

ap (W) - son of.

Apaunaris Civitas (L) - In Devonshire.

app. - apprentice (q. v.); *approximately.

App. Div. - Appelate Divi-

sion.

Appellate Court - Court of Appeals. Abbr. - App.

appr. - appraisment.

apprd. - *appeared.

apprd. - *apprised.

apprentice - one who is bound by indentures or by legal agreement to serve another person for a certain time, with the view to learning an art or a trade. Abbr. - app.

apprs. - *apprisers.

apud (L) - at; by; near; with; among; in; before; in the time of.

a quo (L) - of or from whom

ar (Sw) - year.

a.r. - anno regni (q.v.).

Araldus (L) - Harold.

Aramis, Aranus Civitas (L) - Dorsetshire.

arbiter - judge, umpire.

archaic script - handwriting, or characters used in handwriting, belonging to or having the characteristics of an earlier or more primative time.

archdeacon - the chief deacon. Abbr. - Archd; *arches (pl.).

archdeaconry - the office state, tenure or residence of the archdeacon; a subdivision of a diocese (Church of England). Abbr. - * AD; *adcon.

arches. - *archdeacons (q.

v.).

archididascalus (L) -headmaster.

archives - places in which public records or historic documents are kept; public records or documents preserved as evidence of facts.

archivist - a custodian of archives or records.

Arcturus, Artorius (L) - Arthur.

ardal (W) - country.

arg. - argentum (q.v.).

argentum (L) (Her.) - silver.

Ariz. - Arizona.

Ark. - Arkansas.

armifer (L) - bearing arms or weapons; shield bearer.

armiger - formerly, an armorbearer, as of a knight; an esquire. Later, one next in degree to a knight, and entitled to armorial bearings.

armiger(i) (L) - an armour bearer.

armigerous - bearing (heraldic) arms.

arms - the hereditary ensigns armorial of a family, consisting of figures and colors borne in shields, banners, etc., as marks of dignity and distinction. (GGR, pp. 217-223).

Arn. (Ic) - Arnessysla.

A.R.R. - Anno Regina Regis (q.v.).

arrière grand-mère (Fr) - great-grandmother.

arrière grand-père (Fr) - great-grandfather.

2me arrière grand-père (Fr) - 2nd great-grand father.

3me arrière grand-père (Fr) - 3rd great-grand father.

4me arrière grand-père (Fr) - 4th great-grandfather.

arrière petite-fille (Fr) - great-granddaughter.

arrière petit-fils (Fr) - great-grandson.

arrondissement (Fr) - division of a department or county (in Belgium a county; unit for the registration of vital statistics).

arrondissement (Ne) - civil district.

ascendant - an ancestor (opposed to descendant).

A. Skaft. (Ic) - Austur Skaftafellssysla.

A. Sonbg. (D) - Aabenraa Sønderborg.

asr. - assessor.

atavus (L) - great great grandfather's father; third great grandfather; ancestor.

atque (L) - and; and also or

even; and too; as much as
if; than; yet; nevertheless.

atqui (L) - but; yet; not-
withstanding; however;
rather.

attest - to bear witness to;
to certify; to affirm to be
true or genuine.

attorney, letter of - see
power of attorney.

atturnatus (L) - attorney.

atty. - attorney.

aud.- auditor.

Augusta Trinobantum, Au-
gusta (L) - London.

Augustinus (L) - Austin.

authentic - having a gen-
uine origin or authority,
as opposed to one that is
false, fictitious, counter-
feit, or apocryphal; gen-
uine.

autobiography-a biography
written by the subject of
it; memoirs of one's life
written by oneself.

a.v. - annos vixit (q.v.).

ava, avola (It) - grand-
mother.

avia (L) - grandmother.

aviomies (Fi) - husband.

avioton (Fi) - illegitimate.

avo, avola (It) - grand-
father.

Avona Mediterranea, sive
Borealis (L)-Northamp-
ton.

avunculus (L) - (maternal)
uncle.

avunculus major (L) -

grandmother's brother;
granduncle.

avus (L) -grandfather; ancestor.

az., azure (Her.) - blue.

B

b. - born; *birth; bachelor
(q.v.); brother (q.v.).

ba. - *baptized (q.v.).

baban (W) - infant.

baby (Du) - infant.

bach. - bachelor (q.v.).

bachelor - a knight who followed the standard of an-
other, either because of
his youth or of having too
few vassals of his own;
a man who has not mar-
ried. Abbr. - b.; bach;
*bachr.

bachgen (W) - boy.

bachr. - *bachelor (q.v.).

bad(Ger)-Bath, Spa, health
resort.

baer (Ic) - city.

bambino (It) - infant.

banns - a notice of a pro-
posed marriage, pro-
claimed in a church or
other place prescribed by
law, in order that anyone
may object, if he knows
any impediment to the
marriage. Also - bans;
banns of matrimony.

bans - see banns.

bap. - baptized (q.v.).

baptisata; baptisatus (L) -

baptized.

baptisma; baptisus (L) – baptism.

baptized – having had the rite of baptism. Abbr.– *ba.; bap.; bapt.; *bp.

baptizo (L) – baptize.

barbatus (L) – bearded; adult.

barn (D) (No) (Sw) – child.

barnebarn (D) – grandchild.

barne-barn (No) – grandchild.

barne-barnsbarn (No) – great-grandchild.

barne-barns gutt (No) – great-grandson.

barne-barns pike (No) – great-granddaughter.

barnlös (Sw) – childless.

barnløs (D) childless.

baron – orig., one of a class of tenants in chief of the king or other feudal superior holding by military or other honorable service. Later, baron became restricted to the King's barons who were summoned to the council by writ; a nobleman. Heraldry, a husband as, baron and feme – husband and wife. (see feudal system).

baronet – hereditary title of Sir, in UK. Abbr. – bart, bt.

bart. – baronet (q.v.).

Bartholomeus (L) – Bartholomew.

Base (G) – cousin.

baseborn – of low parentage; born out of wedlock.

bastard–a "natural" child; a child begotten and born out of wedlock.

battesaro (It) – baptized.

battesimo (It) – baptism.

Balt.; *Balto. – Baltimore.

Baudwinus (L) – Baldwin.

bäuerlich (G) – peasantlike.

bautizado (Sp) – baptized.

B.C. – before Christ (67 B.C. = 67 years before Christ).

B.C. – British Columbia.

bcer. – *birthcertificate.

bd. – *birthdate.

B.-du-Rh. (Fr) – Bouches-du-Rhône.

bearing – (usually plural) any single emblem or charge in an escutcheon or coat of arms (qq.v.).

Bearrokscira (L) – Berkshire.

Beatricia, Beatrix (L) – Beatrice.

bedaget (D) – aged.

Beddeford (L) – Bedfordshire.

Bedeforda (L) – Bedford.

Bedfordia (L) – Bedford.

Beds. (E) – Bedford.

bedstefader (D) – grandfather.

bedstemofer (D) – grandmother.

bedyddiwyd (W) - baptized.

bef. - *before.

begraven (Du) (G) - buried.

begravet (D) (No) - buried.

bejaard, oud (Du) - aged, old.

Belg. - Belgium.

ben (Heb) - son.

bene quiescat (L) - may he rest well. Abbr. - b.q.

benyw (W) - woman (in So. Wales).

bequest - act of bequeathing, or leaving by will; also, that which is left by will.

Berceia (L) - Berkshire.

Bercheria (L) - Berkshire.

Berkeia (L) - Berkshire.

Berkeria (L) - Berkshire.

Berks. (E) - Berkshire.

beste-far (No) - grandfather.

beste-foreldre (No) - grandfather and grandmother, grandparents.

bestemor (No) - grandmother.

bet. - *between.

bet-overgrootvader (Du) - 2nd great-grandfather.

bet-over-overgrootvader (Du) - 3rd great-grandfather.

bet-over-over-overgrootvader (Du) - 4th great-grandfather.

bezirk (Sz) - county.

B'ham - *Birmingham.

bibliography - the description of books and manuscripts, with the notices of editions, dates of printing, etc.

biennium - a period of two years.

bill of sale - a formal instrument for the conveyance or transfer of title to goods and chattels.

biography-the written history of a person's life.

bis-a duplicate; repetition a replica.

bis (L) - twice; in a two-fold manner.

bisabuela (Sp) - great-grandmother.

bisabuelo (Sp) - great-grandfather.

bisava (It) - great-grand-daughter.

bisavo (It) - great-grandfather.

biskopsstift - see stift.

bisnieta (Sp) - great-grand-daughter.

bisnieto (Sp) - great-grandson.

bk. - book.

Blestium (L) - Monmouth.

blwyddyn (W) - year.

bndsmn. - *bondsman (q.v.)

bo. - *born; *bought; *bottom.

bona fied - in good faith; without fraud.

bondsman - a slave; villein; serf; a surety on a bond; one who is bound for another. Abbr. *bndsnm.

bonedd (W) – pedigree.

bonus (L) – good; kind; high; honourable.

Borg. (Ic) –Borgarfjardar-sysla.

Bornhm. (D) – Bornholm.

borough–among the Anglo-Saxons, the enclosure protecting a house; a fortified house; a fortified group of houses; later; a town, or urban constituency sharing in the election of a member or members to Parliament.

b.o.t.p.–both of this parrish.

bounty land warrant – a right granted for military service involving a specific number of acres of unallocated public land. (ABC p. 75; SR p. 19).

bovate – an obsolete English unit of land measure, varying from 7 to 32 acres.

Boyd's Marriage Index –an index to many of the early marriages of England.

bp. – *baptized (q.v.).

bpl. – place of birth.

b.q. – bene quiescat (q.v.).

Br. – British.

br.; bro; – brother (q.v.).

Brabant. (Bel) – Brabant.

brand – a mark of identification burned into the flank or side of an animal to show ownership. Brands have been registered for many years and may assist genealogists as they were very often hereditary. See earmark.

Brandbg. (G) – Brandenburg.

brawd (W) – brother.

B.Rhin (Fr) – Bas Rhin.

Brigida, Brigitta (L) – Bridget.

Brit. – British, Britian.

bro. – brother.

bro (W) – country.

broder, bror (D) –brother.

broder (Sw) – brother.

broderdatter (D) – brother's daughter (niece).

brodersøn (D) – brother's son (nephew).

broeder (Du) – brother.

bro-i-l; bro-il.; bro. il. – *brother-in-law (q.v.).

bror (No) – brother.

brorsdotter (Sw) – brother's daughter (niece).

brorson (Sw) – brother's son (nephew).

brother – son of your father & mother; one of a common family; in a more general sense, a fellow man. Abbr. – b.; br.; bro. (see SYA p. 140 for instability of use).

brother-in-law–husband of your wife's sister; husband of your sister. Abbr. *bro-i-l.; *bro. il.;

*bro.-i-l. (See SYA p. 140).

bruder (G) - brother.

Brunsw. (G) - Brunswick (Braunschweig).

Bses-Alpes (Fr) - Basses-Alpes.

Bses-Pyr. (Fr) - Basses-Pyrenees.

bt. - baronet (q.v.).

Bu. - Abu (q.v.).

Buckingeham (L) - Buckinghamshire.

Buckinghamia (L) - Buckingham.

Bucks. (E) - Buckingham.

Budiforda (L) - Bedford.

buitenechelijk (Du) - illegitimate.

bur. - *buried, burial.

burg (G) - castle.

Burgenld. (Aus) - Burgenland.

burgher registers - registers maintained as proof of citizenship in a given town in Switzerland. (GGR p. 262).

Buskd. (No) - Buskerud.

bustum (L) - tomb, sepulchral.

by (D) - city, town.

by (No) - small town, village.

C

c.; ca.; circa. - about (or around a certain year.)

ca. - circa (q.v.).

cadastral survey, map, or plan - a survey, map or plan for making a cadastre. Usually made on a large scale, about a square inch to the acre.

cadastre (er) - an official register of real estate, used in apportioning taxes.

cadaver (L) - dead body; corpse.

cadet (Fr) - youngest.

cado (L) - to be slain; to abate; to decay; to end; to fail.

Caecilia (L) - Cecily.

Caecilius (L) - Cecil.

caedes (L) - slaughter; murder; persons slain or murdered.

caelebs, coelebs (L) - unmarried.

Caerns. (W) - Caernarvon.

Caith. (Sc) - Caithness.

Caius (L) - Kay.

Cajun - corruption of Arcadian; in La. descendant of an Arcadian.

calendar, Old Style - see Julian calendar; double dating.

calendared - when records are arranged chronologically.

calends - the first day of the Roman month; a calendar; a record; a register.

Calif. - California.

call number – the number assigned a book in a library, used when calling or asking for the same.

calo (L) – soldier's boy; low servant.

Camboricum, Camborium (L) – Cambridge.

Cambs. (E) – Cambridge.

canon – a decree, decision, regulation, code or constitution made by ecclesiastical authority; a law, or rule of doctrine or discipline, enacted by a council and confirmed by the Pope or the sovereign.

Cantabrigia (L) – Cambridgeshire.

Cantia, Cantium (L) – Kent.

canton – a small territorial division of a country; one of the states of the Swiss Confederation; a rectangular division of the shield, used in modern heraldry for the diminutive of the old quarter.

canton (Fr) – county in Switzerland; sub-division of an arrondissement. (in Belgium a district under the jurisdiction of a Judge of Peace).

canus (L) – hoary, gray; foamy; old age.

caput (L) – head; source; life; person; intelligence; chief.

card catalogue – a catalogue, list or index of the books and other material of a library entered on cards. Most genealogical libraries have a surname catalogue and a place or geographical catalogue. Also–card index.

Cards. (W) – Cardigan.

Carms. (W) – Carmarthen.

Carolus (L) – Charles.

carucate – about 120 acres. Probably other meanings.

casado (Sp) – married.

cath. – cathed.

cath. – cathedral (q.v.).

cathedral – the principal church of a diocese. Abbr. – cath.

causidicus (L) – barrister; advocate.

C-du-N. (Fr) – Côtes du Nord.

cefn der (W) – male cousin.

célibataire (Fr) – unmarried.

cem. – *cemetery.

cen. – *census.

censeo (L) – to count; to reckon; to tax, to vote.

census – a official enumeration of the population of a country, city or other administrative district, with statistics of commerce, wealth and social conditions; a tax, esp. a poll tax.

census records or returns -the records compiled by the census takers and kept mostly by the Bureau of Census.

census (L) - valuation of every Roman Citizen's estate; mustering of the people.

cer. - *certificate.

cerca de (Sp) - about.

Cernualia, Curnualia (L)- Cornwall.

certified copy-a copy made or attested by officers having charge of the original and authorized to give copies.

certified extract - in genealogy, a certified copy of parts of a document, such as a will, giving only the information pertaining to relationships, locations, etc.

Cestria (L) - Chester.

Cestrisria (L) - Cheshire.

cf., confer; (L) - compare.

ch. - church; child; children; chief.

ch(s). - church(es).

CH - Courthouse.

chan. - chancery.

chapelry - the territorial district assigned to a chapel; the chapel with all its apurtenances (records, etc.) (see GGR p. 223).

charge (Her) - to place a bearing on a shield, etc.

Char Marit. (Fr) - Charente Maritime.

checky (Her) - checked or checkered; of a field or charge - divided into rectangles of alternate tinctures.

Ches. (E) - Cheshire.

Chestria, Chestrum (L) - Chester.

ch/o - *child of.

chr. - christened (q.v.).

chris. - *christened.

Christened - to receive or initate into the visible church of Christ by baptism; to baptize; to name at baptism; to give a name to.

Christopherus (L) - Christopher.

churching(e)s - administration or reception of a rite by which one is churched; specif: a ceremony by which, after childbirth, women are received in the church with prayers, blessings and thanksgiving.

churchyard - the yard or enclosure belonging to a church part of which is often used as a burial ground; God's acre.

chwaer (W) - sister.

cir. - circa; circum (qq.v.).

circ. - circa; circum (qq.v).

circa (L) - about; near to.

Abbr. - c.; ca.; cir.; circ.

circiter; circum (L) - about; near; towards. Abbr. - c.; cir.; circ.

città (It) - city, town.

city - a large important town; U.S.; an incorporated municipality; Canada: a municipality of high rank, usually based on population; British: a borough, usually the seat of a bishop, upon which the dignity of the title has been conferred by the Crown.

ciudad (Sp) - city, town.

ciuitate (L) - city.

civ. - civil.

civicus (L) - civic; civil; pertaining to the Roman state.

civil law - the laws of a state or nation regulating ordinary private matters (distinguished from criminal, military, or political matters); the body of law proper to the city or state of Rome, as distinct from that common to all nations; the systems of law derived from Roman law (distinguished from common law, cannon law).

Clack. (Sc) - Clackmannan.

claddwyd (W) - buried.

clan - a group of people of common descent.

Claudia, Claudia Castra (L) - Gloucester.

Claudiana provincia (L) - Gloucestershire.

Claudiocestria (L) - Gloucester.

Cleocestria (L) - Gloucester.

Clevum (L) - Gloucester.

clk. - clerk.

cloister; cloyster (L) - a monastery or convent.

co. - county (q.v.); Company.

coat of arms - a surcoat or tabard embroidered with heraldic devices, worn by medieval knights over their armor; the heraldic bearings of a person; the hatchment; an escutcheon. (GGR 217-223).

codicil - a supplement to a will, modifying, adding to or changing it; In Roman, canon and early English law a kind of informal will made without the appointment of executors said to be essential to a formal will.

coelebs (L) - single.

cognate - related by birth; of the same parentage, descent, etc.; related on the mother's side.

cognatus (L) - related by birth; kinsman; kinswoman.

cognomen (L) – family name; epithet; the Roman name corresponding to our surname.

c.o.h.; coh. –*coheir (q.v.).

coheir; coheiress – a joint heir. Abbr. –*coh.; c.o.h.

col.–colony; colonel.

coll. – college; collections.

collateral ancestors – belonging to the same ancestral stock but not in direct line of descent; opposed to lineal; father and son are lineal, uncles, aunts, cousins, etc., are collateral kinsman.

collateral lines – persons descending from collateral kinsman.

College of Arms – Heralds' College (q.v.).

College of Heralds – Heralds' College (q.v.).

Colo. – Colorado.

colona (L) – country woman.

colonus (L) – husbandman, farmer.

com. – *comitatus; *county (qq.v.); commissioner; commander; commentary; committee; common; commoner; communicate.

comitatus (L) – English county; escort; train, retinue; company; troop. Abbr. – *com.

comm.– commissioners.

common law – a system of law originating in England, as distinct from the civil or Roman Law and the canon or ecclesiastical law; the unwritten law.

common–law–marriage – a marriage without ceremony, civil or ecclesiastical. Recognized at times in some places, mostly unrecognized.

commoner – a citizen or burgess; one of a town council; one of the common people, having no rank of nobility.

communicant – one who partakes of, or is entitled to partake of, the sacrament of the Lord's Supper; a church member.

comp. – *company.

compar (L) – alike, equal; comrade; lover, consort.

compt (L) – county.

comte (Fr) – county.

con. – conjunx (q.v.).

condado (Sp) – county.

condito (L) – condition; situation; agreement; marriage; married person.

confirmation – in various churches: a rite supplemental to baptism.

coniugal (It) – married.

conjugium (L) – marriage; wedlock; husband.

conjunx (L) – wife. Abbr. –

con.

conjux (L) - spouse; wife; bride; husband.

Conn. - Connecticut.

consanguineus (L) - related by blood; brotherly; sisterly.

consanguinity - state of being related by blood, or descended from a common ancestor.

consobrina (L) - first cousin on the father's side.

consobrinus (L) - (female) cousin-german (on the mother's side).

consort - a partner, companion, or collegue; a wife or husband; spouse; mate. (SYA 79).

Constantia (L) - Constance.

cont. - continued; contract.

contea (It) - county.

contemporary records - records written or compiled at the time the event occured; records originating or recorded in the same period.

contr. - *contrast; contract.

Cophgn. (D) - Copenhagen.

copulerede (D) - married.

copyholder - one who holds his land as a tenant by copy of the court roll.

Corinea (L) - Cornwall.

Corn. (E) - Cornwall. Cornish.

Cornuallia, Cornubia (L) - Cornwall.

corp. - corporal.

corpus (L) body, substance; flesh; corpse.

Cos. - Counties.

couns. - *counsellor.

county - an earldom; the domain of a count or earl. In Great Britain and Northern Ireland one of the territorial divisions constituting the chief units for administrative, judicial and political purposes. The first districts to be called counties were the old Anglo Saxon shires, often called the ancient, or geographical counties, or, more commonly, counties at large, which had various historical origins going back to Anglo-Saxon days. Later the term was applied to: 1. Certain districts consisting of towns or cities with neighboring territory separated out of the older shires and given the organization of counties (and called counties corporate or corporate counties). 2. Certain duchies (as Cornwall, Shetland, etc.). 3. Administrative divisions (often not coincident with the older counties) to which the administrative functions (but not the judicial or political ones) of the older counties have been transferred under the Local Government Act of 1888 and which are called administrative counties. In Scotland, the 33 civil counties into which the country is divided, is substantially the same as that of England. In the U.S., it is the largest division of local government in all the states except Louisiana, where the corresponding division is the parish. Abbr. - Co.; co.; ct.; Latin - *com.

county palatine - dominion or territory of a count or earl palatine. In England, county of which the earl or county had originally royal powers with exclusive civil and criminal jurisdiction. (now abolished.)

county town - an English town which is the seat of county administration.

court docket - see trial docket.

cous. - *cousin (q.v.).

cous-i-l. - cousin-in-law (q.v.).

cousin - anyone collaterally related more remotely than a brother or sister; a son or daughter of one's own uncle or aunt (called more fully own, first, or full cousin, or cousin-german); paternal cousin - on the father's side; maternal cousin - on the mother's side. (see relationship chart for detailed cousin relationship) Cousin is sometimes used in a general sense as a sort of title of endearment even when there is no blood relationship. Abbr. - *cous.

cousin; cousine (Fr) - cousin.

cousin-german - first cousin; a son or daughter of your father's or mother's brother or sister.

cousin-in-law - one married to a cousin. Abbr. - *cous-i-l.

C.P. - Cape of Good Hope, know as Cape Province. (So. Africa.)

C.R. - *church record.

crest - a bearing or device set not upon the shield but on the helm, and used separately as an ornament or cognizance for plate, liveries, and the like. (see bearings, shield, coat of arms, arms).

crim. - criminal.

croft - a small agriculture holding worked by a

peasant.

crofter - one who rents or tills a croft (q.v.).

crspd. - *correspond; *correspondence.

csn. - *cousin; *cousins.

ct. - court; county.

cuadro genealógico (Sp) - pedigree chart.

cuis susceptores (L) - godparents.

cugina (It) - female cousin.

cugino (It) - male cousin.

cugino germano (It) - first cousin.

cum (L) - with; along with; under; in; by.

Cumb. (E) - Cumberland.

Cumberlandia, Cumbria (L) - Cumberland.

curate - one who is a deputy of a rector or vicar (qq.v.).

Curnualia (L) - Cornwall.

CW. - *Civil War.

cyfnither (W) -female cousin.

cyndad (W) - ancestor.

C.Z. - Territory of Canal Zone.

D

D. - Dutch.

d. - date; daughter (q.v.); day; days; dead; died; *death.

da. - daughter (q.v.); day; days.

dag-(D) (Du) (No) (Sw) day.

Dal. (Ir) - Dalasysla.

Damnonia (L) -Devonshire.

Dan. - Danish; Denmark (Danmark).

D. & C. - Dean and Chapter (q.v.).

d & coh. - *daughter and coheiress (q.v.).

d. & h. - daughter and heiress (q.v.).

D&W - *Deed & Wills.

dans l énfance (Fr) -infant.

D.A.R. - Daughters of the American Revolution (q. v.).

Darbia (L) - Derby.

dates, double - see doubledating.

dator (L) - giver.

datter (D) (No) - daughter.

datterdatter (D) - daughter's daughter (granddaughter).

datter-datter (No) -daughter's daughter (granddaughter).

Dattersøn (D) - daughter's son (grandson).

datter-sønn (No) - daughter's son (grandson).

dau. - daughter (q.v.).

daughter - one's female child; also used as a title of endearment for any female, whether there be blood relationship or not. Abbr. - d.; da.; dau.; *daugr.; *dt. (see SYA p. 140).

daughter-in-law - the wife

of one's son. Abbr. dau-i-l. (see SYA p. 140).

Daughters of the American Revolution - a patriotic society of American women, organized to preserve the memory of those active in achieving American independence. Abbr. D.A.R.

Daughters of the Revolution - a patriotic society of woman, similar to D.A.R. Abbr. - D.R.

daugr. - *daughter (q.v.).

dau-i-l - *daughter-in-law (q.v.).

daus. - daughters.

D.B. - *Domesday Book (q.v.).

D.C. - Dist of Columbia.

de (L) - down from; from; out of; about; at; for; etc.

dea. - deacon.

deac. - *deacon.

dean - a chief or head of ten men; hence, a tithingman; a head over ten monks in a monastery; the head of the chapter, or body of canons or prebendaries. (see Dean and Chapter).

Dean and Chapter - Constitutes the legal corporation of the church. The dean is the head of the chapter which is a regular assembly of the canons of a cathedral or a collegiate church, or of the members of other religious orders. Abbr.-D. and C.

deanery - the office, position or official residence of the dean; a subdivision of an archdeaconry. Also Rural Deanery. Several parishes make a deanery.

death notice - in some countries, the notice of death filed with the probate court with or without a will, giving considerable genealogical information.

dec.; decd; dec'd. - deceased.

décédé, décédée (Fr) - died

décédé sans posterite (Fr) - died without issue.

decedent - a deceased person.

decessit sine prole (L) - he died without issue. Abbr. - d.s.p.

decessit vita matris (L) - he died in his mother's lifetime. Abbr. - *d.v.m.

decessit vita patris (L) - he died in his father's lifetime. Abbr. - d.v.p.

decido (L) - to fall down; to die.

Declaration of Intention - a sworn statement by an alien that he intends to become a citizen.

deed of indenture - see

indenture.

deed - a sealed instrument in writing, on paper or parchment, duly executed and delivered, containing some transfer, bargain, or contract; also loosely, such an instrument before it has been given effect by delivery. In its broadest sense deed properly included every such instrument; but it is often used specifically of an instrument conveying a fee of land, as distinguished from a mortgage, lease or other instruments under seal. A will although under seal is not a deed, because not delivered and accepted.

deforceant - defendant.

defunct - dead.

degener (L) - degenerate; lowborn; base.

Del. - Delaware.

De La, De Le, Del (Norman Fr) - all mean "from the" followed by a place.

Den. - Denmark.

Dena Victrix (L) - Chester.

Denb. (W) - Denbigh.

denizen - an inhabitant; an alien admitted to residence.

denomino (L) - to name; to call.

denicalis (L) - solemn purification of a house, on the tenth day after the death of a person.

denubo (L) - to marry; to marry beneath one's condition.

Deorbeia (L) - Derby.

department (Fr) - county or province in France.

depose - say under oath; testify.

deposition - a testifying or testimony taken down in writing under oath of affirmation in reply to interrogatories, before a competent officer to replace the viva voce (oral) testimony of the witness.

Derby. (E) - Derbyshire.

Derebiscira (L) - Derbyshire.

Derry (Ire) - Londonderry.

desc. - descendant (q.v.).

descendant - one who descends, as an offspring, however remotely; opposed to ancestor, ascendent. Abbr. - desc.

Deutsch (G) - German.

Deuna (L) - Chester.

Deva, Devana, Devania (L) - Chester.

devisee - a person to whom lands or other real property are devised or given by will.

devisor - a giver of lands or real estate by will; a testator.

Devon. (E) – Devonshire.

Devonia (L) – Devonshire.

dft.– defendant.

dí (It) – day.

dia (Sp) – day.

dibriod (W) – unmarried.

dico (L) – to tell; to order; to call; to plead; etc.

die (L) – see dies.

died without issue – died without having children.

dies (L) – day; daylight; day of burial. Abbr. – d.

dinas (W) – city.

dio. – *diocese (q.v.).

diocése (Fr) – bishopric, presided over by a bishop.

diocese – the administrative division of a country; esp., a division of the prefecture of the Roman Empire; the circuit or extent of a bishop's jurisdiction; the district in which a bishop has authority. Abbr. – *dio.

discidium (L) separation; divorce.

disinherit – to cut off from, or deprive of, an inheritance or hereditary succession.

dist. – district.

distribution –the apportionment, by a court, of the personal property of an intestate among those entitled to it.

District Land Office Plat Book – books or rather maps which show the location of the land of the patentee. (see patent; also ABC p. 76).

District Land Office Tract Books – books which list individual entries by range and township. (ABC p. 76).

div. – divorced.

Divana (L) – Chester.

diwrnod (W) – day.

do. – ditto; the same.

d/o – *daughter of.

døbt (D) – baptized.

doc. – document; doctor.

dochter (Du) – daughter.

document – an original or official paper relied upon as the basis, proof or support of anything.

documented history – a history which has as its basis documents, such as certified, photostat or originals copied verbatim (see legal and historical methods).

død (D) – died.

døde (No) – died.

døde barnløs (No) – died without issue.

døduden afkom (D) – died without issue.

död utan bröstarvinge (Sw) – died without issue.

dom. – domestic.

Domesday Book – the ancient record of the Grand, or Great Inquest or Survey of the lands of England, made 1085-86 by order of William the Conqueror. It consists of two volumes sometimes called the Little Domesday and the Great Domesday. The Domesday Book gives a census-like description of the realm, with the names of the proprietors, the nature, extent value, liabilities, etc., of their properties. Abbr. - *D.B.

domina (L) - mistress of a family; lady; wife.

dominus (L) - master of the house; owner; ruler; "Sir".

Domnania (L) - Devonshire.

domsaga (Sw) - judicial district or circuit.

domus (L) - house; home; family; native country; temple.

donation application - application for frontier land in Florida, New Mexico, Oregon or Washington. Given to an actual settler upon certain conditions. (see ABC p. 75; SR p. 19).

donation lands - see donation application.

donee - one to whom a gift is made.

donor - a person who makes a gift.

döpt (Sw) - baptized.

Dorbeia (L) - Derby.

Dorcestria (L) - Dorsetshire.

dorf (G) (Sz) - village.

Dorothea (L) - Dorothy.

dorp (Ne) - village.

Dorset. (E) - Dorsetshire.

Dorsetania, Dorsetia (L) - Dorsetshire.

dött (Sw) - died.

dotter (Sw) - daughter.

dotterdotter (Sw) - daughter's daughter (granddaughter).

dotterson (Sw) - daughter's son (grandson).

double-dating - a system of double-dating was used in England and America from 1582 to 1752 because it was not clear as to whether the year commenced on Jan. 1 or March 25. The new Gregorian Calendar (q.v.) year started Jan. 1 and the old Julian (q.v.) year started on March 25. Double-dating is very common during the years 1582 to Sept. 2, 1752 but was only necessary from Jan. 1 to March 24 of each year. During this period most dates were written similar to this: 25 Jan. 1744/5, indicating that the year was 1744 by the old style or Julian Calendar and 1745 by the new style or Gregorian Calendar. However, some of the churches did not recognize the new style and care must be used in figuring dates of this period. From March 25 to Dec. 31 the year was the same on both calendars so no double dates were necessary. (see G GR pp. 320-330; ABC p. 90; 1953 HB p. 220).

dower - that portion of, or interest in, the real estate of a deceased husband which the law gives to his widow during her life; the property which a woman brings to a husband in marriage - now usually called dowery.

døpt (No) - baptized.

dpl. - *place of death.

D.R. - Daughters of the Revolution (q.v.).

dragoon - ancient carbine; dragon; a mounted infantryman armed with a dragoon.

dreng, drengebarn (D) - boy, male child.

Drente. (Ne) - Drenthe.

d.s. - document signed.

dsct. - *descendant.

D./ Sevres (Fr) - Deux/ Sevres.

d.s.p. - decessit sine prole (q.v.).

dt. - *daughter (q.v.).

Du. - Dutch.

duco (L) - to marry; to take; to bring; to persuade; etc.

Dumf. (Sc) - Dumfries.

Dumnonia (L) - Devonshire.

Dunb. (Sc) - Dunbarton.

Dunholmus, Dunholmum (L) - Durham.

Duria (L) - Dorsetshire.

dux (L) - leader; guide.

duxit (L) - married; husband.

d.v.m. - * decessit vita matris (q.v.).

d.v.p. - decessit vita patris (q.v.).

dwt. - pennyweight(s).

d.y. - *died young.

dydd (W) - day.

dyn (W) - man.

dynes (W) - woman.

E

e. - east or eastern.

ead. - *eadem (q.v.).

eadem (L) - in the same way. Abbr. - *ead.

Eadmundus (L) - Edmund.

Eadwardus (L) - Edward.

earl - among the Anglo-Saxons, a warrior, esp. one of noble rank; a man; the viceroy of one of the four great divisions of England; a nobleman ranking below a marquis, and above a viscount.

earmark - a mark of identification on the ear of an animal, usually used in connection with a brand to identify ownership. Earmarks and brands (q.v.) were registered and sometimes assist genealogists as they were quite often passed from father to son.

East-Sexena (L) - Essex.

Eboracum (L) - York.

Ebor'scira (L) - Yorkshire.

Eburacum (L) - York.

ecclesia (L) - church.

echtgenoot (Du) - husband.

echtgenote (Du) - wife.

ed. - edited; edition; editor.

edad (Sp) - age.

Editha (L) - Edith.

editicius (L) - named; allowed.

educ. - education or educated.

E./er/L. (Fr) - Eure/et/Loir.

E. Fland. (Bel) - Oost Vlaanderen.

e.g. - exempli gratia (L. for example).

Egidius (L) - Giles.

ego (L) - I, I myself; house; family.

ehefrau (G) - wife.

ehemann (G) - husband.

ei ferch (W) - daughter, his daughter.

Einwohner-Meldeamt (Sz)

(G) - citizen s registration office.

ej. - *ejus (q.v.).

ejus (L) - his; hers; of him; (filius ejus - son of him; uxor ejus - wife of him). Abbr. - *ej.

Eleanora (L) - Eleanor.

Elena (L) - Ellen.

Elisabetha (L) - Elizabeth, Isabella.

el mayor (Sp) - eldest.

el menor (Sp) - youngest.

E. Lothian (Sc) - East Lothian.

elst (No) - eldest.

elugeo (L) - to mourn the full time.

Emelina (L) - Emily.

emigrant - one departing from a country to settle permanently elsewhere. (see immigrant).

emigration records - the records made of persons leaving a country (see GGR pp. 34-37).

emorior (L) - to die; to perish; to cease.

en bas âge (Fr) - infant.

enfant (Fr) - child.

Eng. - England; English.

enke (D) (No) - widow.

enkel (G) - grandson.

enkelin (G) - granddaughter.

enkemand (D) - widower.

enkemann (No) - widower.

eno. - *enough.

Ens. - Ensign.

enseveli, ensevelie (Fr) -

buried.

enteré, enterrée (Fr) – buried.

enterrado (Sp) – buried.

entry – the act of making or entering a record; that which is entered.

enubo (L) – to marry out of one's rank; to marry and leave the paternal house.

enumeration – a census (q.v.).

enumerator – one who counts or lists; the census taker.

enuptio (L) – marrying out of one's rank.

enutrio (L) – to nourish; to bring up.

eo (L) – thither; so far; to go; to walk; there; etc.

eodem (L) – to the same place or purpose.

eodem die – same day.

Ep. – Episcopus (q.v.).

Episcopus (L) – bishop. Abbr. – Ep.; Epus.

epitaph – an inscription on or at a tomb or grave in memory of the one buried there.

epitaphium (L) – funeral oration.

épouse (Fr) – wife.

époux (Fr) – husband.

E. Pruss. (G) – Ostpreussen.

Epus. – Episcopus (q.v.).

ergo (L) – wherefore; therefore; then; now.

erratum (L) – error, mistake. (pl. errata).

escheat – the process whereby property was forfeited to the Crown in England and to the State in U.S.

escutcheon – the variously shaped surface, usually a sheild, on which armorial bearings are depicted, marshaled and displayed. (see GGR p. 217; also heraldry).

esi–isá (Fi) – ancestor.

esikoinen (Fi) – firstborn.

esposa (Sp) – wife.

esposo (Sp) – husband.

Essexa (L) – Essex.

est. – *estate; *established

estates in litigation – estates left with no apparent heir or with no will and going through the judicial process to determine who shall inherit.

estd. – *estimated.

Estsexa (L) – Essex.

et (L) – and; also; yet; etc.

et.al. (L) – et alibi or et alli; and others; and elsewhere. (Look for others).

éta (It) – age.

et seq.; et seqq. (L) – et sequentes, et sequentia; and those that follow.

et ux. – et uxor (q.v.).

et uxor (L) – and wife. Abbr. – et ux.

Everwyk (L) – York.

evidence – that which is submitted as a means of ascertaining the truth of any alleged matter of fact. It may be done by means of witnesses, records, documents, concrete objects, etc., and may be for the purpose of proving or disproving any matter.

evito (L) – to kill.

ewyllys, ewyllys diweddaf (W) – will, testament.

ewyrth, ewyythr (W) –uncle.

ex asse heres (L) – universal or sole heir.

exc. – except; excellency; excepted; exchange.

excerpt – an extract; a passage selected or copied from a book or record.

excessus (L) – departure; death.

Exchequer Rolls –financial account of various sheriffs and their assistants, who collected rents and fines in Great Britain (see GGR p. 261).

excise – any duty, toll or tax; to lay or impose an excise upon.

exciseman – an officer who inspects and rates articles liable to excise duty.

ex, e (before consonants) (L) – out of; from; down from; after, etc.

exec. – executor (q.v.).

executor – the person appointed by a testator to execute his will, or to see its provisions carried into effect, after his decease; the personal representative of the testator (q.v.). Abbr. – exec.; *exec.; exors.

executrix – a woman exercising the functions of an executor. Abbr. – * exox.

exeo (L) – to go out or away; to escape; to end; to die.

Exexa (L) – Essex.

exhalo (L) – to breath out; to evaporate; to die.

exheres (L) – disinherited; disinherited person.

exor; – *executor (q.v.).

exorior (L) – to arise; to begin; to originate.

exors – *executors (q.v.).

exox. – *executrix (q.v.).

exr. – executor (q.v.).

exrx. – excutrix (q.v.).

exscribo (L) – to write off; to copy.

exsequialis (L) – funeral.

exspiro (L) – to breath out; to exhale; to cease; to die.

extract – a selection from a writing; a quotation. (see certified extract).

extra-parochal district – special district with certain independent jurisdictions in England.

exx. - executrix (q.v.).

eyf. (Ir) - Eyjafardarsyla.

F

f. - father (q.v.); feast; feet; feminine; form; folio; following; foot; for; etc.

faber (L) - artisan; workman; smith; carpenter.

fabricator (L) - artificer; farmer; contriver.

facsimile - an exact and detailed copy of anything.

faddere (D) - witnesses.

fader (Sw) - father.

fader, far (D) - father.

Faero. (D) - Faerøerne.

falleció (Sp) - died.

fam. - family or families.

familia (L) - family; servants or slaves belonging to one master; household; sect.

famula (L) - female slave; maid-servant.

famulus (L) - slave, servant; attendant.

fanciullo (It) - child.

far (No) - father.

farbroder (D) - father's brother (uncle).

farbror (Sw) - father's brother (uncle).

farfar (D) (No) (Sw) - father's father (grandfather).

farfars far (Sw) - father's father's father (great-grandfather).

farfars mor (Sw) - father's father's mother (great-grandmother).

farmor (D) (No) (Sw) - father's mother (grandmother).

farmors far (Sw) - father's mother's father (great-grandfather).

farmors mor (Sw) - father's mother's mother (great-grandmother).

fars farbror (Sw) - father's father's brother (granduncle).

fars faster (Sw) - father's father's sister (grandaunt).

fars morbror (Sw) - father's mother's brother (granduncle).

fars moster (Sw) - father's mother's sister (grandaunt).

farsøster (D) - father's sister (aunt).

F.A.S.G. - Fellow American Society of Genealogists.

faster (D) - maternal aunt.

faster (Sw) - father's sister (aunt).

father - the nearest male ancestor; any male ancestor; a title of endearment bestowed upon an older, close associate with no blood relationship; a dignitary of the church. Abbr. – f.

father-i-l – *father-in-law.

father-in-law – father of your wife or husband. Abbr. – *father-i-l.

fätter (D) – male cousin.

f.e. – for example.

feast days – a holy day set apart annually for solemn commemoration. In the middle Ages and later many records established their dates from various feast days, some fixed and some movable. (see GGR p 320).

fecerunt (L) – they did it. Abbr. – ff.

fee – an estate of inheritance in land, being either a fee simple or a fee tail (qq. v.); an estate in land held of a feudal lord on condition of the performing of certain services.

fee simple – a fee (q. v.) without limitation to any particular class of heirs or restrictions upon alienation.

fee tail – an estate of inheritance or fee (q. v.) limited to lineal descendant heirs (or heirs of the body) of the person to whom it is granted.

feet of fines – began with the reign of Richard I, of England and were practically deeds transferring land, though nominally the "finis" or end of a fictitious suit; they are of great value to the genealogist, giving minute accounts of land transfers at a date when deeds were exceedingly rare. (see GGR p. 230).

femina (L) – female, woman; she. . . . .

femme (Fr) – wife, woman.

femmina (It) – woman.

feod – feud (q. v.).

fere (L) – nearly; almost; about; very; in general.

Fermanh. (Ire) – Fermanagh.

ferrarius (L) – Ironmonger; relating to or belonging to iron.

Ferulega (L) – Hereford.

fetter (No) – male cousin.

feud – an estate of land held of a feudal lord on condition of the performing of certain services; a territory held in fee (q. v.).

feudal system – the system of polity which prevailed in Europe in the Middle Ages, based upon the relation of lord to vassal, with the holding of the land in feud, fief or fee (qq. v.) (baron).

FF. – Frates (q. v.).

ff. - fecerunt (q.v.); following (pages); ff is also
used in Old English
script as a capitol "F".

F.F.V. - First Families of
Virginia.

f.i. - for instance.

F.I.A.G. - Fellow Institute
of American Genealogy
(defunct).

fid. - fiduciary (q.v.).

fiduciary - a person to
whom property is en-
trusted to hold, control,
or manage for another.
Abbr. - fid.

fief - a feudal estate; a fee;
a feud (qq.v.).

figlia (It) - daughter.

figlio (It) - son.

f-i-l - *father-in-law.

filia (L) - daughter; female
offspring.

filia fratris (L) -brother's
daughter (niece).

filia sororis (L) - sister's
daughter (niece).

filiola (L) - little daughter.

filiolus (L) - little son.

filius (L) - son; male offspring.

filius fratris (L) - brother's
son; nephew.

filius sororis (L) - sister's
son; nephew.

fille (Fr) - daughter, girl.

fils (Fr) - son.

Finist. (Fr) - Finestère.

Finmk. (No) - Finnmark.

fistulator (L) - piper; one

who plays on a reed-pipe.

Fitz (Norman Fr) - a pre-
fix to the father's name,
meaning son.

fixed feast days - see feast
days.

fl. - floruit (q.v.).

Fla. - Florida.

flicka (Sw) - girl.

Flints (W) - Flintshire.

floruit (L) - he flourished.
Abbr. - fl.

född (Sw) - born.

født (D) (No) - born.

fol. - following.

foraeldre (D) - parents.

forfader (D) - forefather,
ancestor.

förfader (Sw) - ancestor.

forsamling (Sw) - church
parish.

förjsfödd (Sw) - firstborn.

førstefødt (D) firstborn, eldest.

fr. - frater (q.v.).

franc - or frei (G) - free.

Franciscus (L) - Francis.

Francus (L) - Frank.

frank - free; not in bond-
age; to exempt from ch-
arge from postage; to en-
able to pass or go freely
or easily.

frank marriage - the tenure
by which a man and his
wife held an estate granted by a blood relative of
the wife in consideration
of their marriage (whe-
ther before or after it)

to be held of the donor by the issue of the marriage to not less than the fourth generation and without other service than faithfulness to the grantor.

franklin - an English freeholder in the 14th & 15th centuries; a middle-class landowner.

Franklin, State of - the area once known as the "State of Franklin" was never officially recognized and was under consideration for only a short time. It is of importance to research in the southern states. Organized 1784 from the western part of North Carolina, ceased to exist 1788. (see ABC p 96).

Franks - members of the confederated German tribes who founded the Franklin Empire which eventually gave place to the medieval kingdoms that became France, Germany and Italy.

fratello (It) - brother.

frater (L) - brother; cousin; brother-in-law; kinsman. Abbr. - fr.

Fratres (L) - Brothers. Abbr. - FF.

fratricida (L) - murder of a brother.

fratris (L) - see frater.

fratris filia - see filia fratris.

frau (G) - woman.

fra will - below 40 pounds (sterling).

Fraxula Flu (L) - In Derbyshire.

Frdbg. (D) - Frederiksborg.

freehold - an estate in fee simple, in fee tail (qq.v.) of for life.

freeman - one who enjoys liberty, or who is not subject to the will of another; not a slave or vassal; one having the freedom of a company or municipality; (see SYA 141).

freeholder - the owner of a freehold.

frei (G) - free.

Freibg. (G) - Freiburg.

frère (Fr) - brother.

Friends - a religious sect with various divisions such as; Society of Friends, Religious Society of Friends, Orthodox Conservative Friends and Primative Friends. They are popularly called Quakers. The minutes of their Monthly Meetings (q.v.) furnish a wealth of genealogical information (see ABC p. 111).

Friesl. (Ne) - Friesland.

F.S.G. - Fellow Society of

Genealogists, (British).

fuit (L) – was.

funebris (L) – funeral; deadly; mortal; cruel.

funereus (L) – funeral; deadly; destructive.

funero (L) – to kill. ruin; death.

furn. – *furniture.

fylker (No) – present term for county, shire.

G

G. – German, Germany.

g. – grand; *great, (qq.v.).

Ga. – Georgia.

gaard (No) – farm or group of several farms.

gaardmand (D) – owner of house and ground, independent farmer.

Galfredus, Gaufridus (L) – Geoffrey.

Galterus (L) – Walter.

gammal (Sw) – old aged.

gammel (D) (No) old, aged.

ganwyd (W) – born.

G.A.R. – Grand Army of the Republic. An organization formed by veterans of the Union who fought in the Civil War.

garcon (Fr) – boy.

gard (Sw) – farm.

gardianus – (L) churchwarden.

gatte (G) – husband.

gattin (G) – wife.

Gavlebg. (Sw) – Gavleborg.

gazetteer – a geographical dictionary; a book giving names and descriptions of places in alphabetical order.

G.B. – Great Britain.

gch.– *grandchildren.

gdn. – *guardian.

geboren (Du) (G) – born.

gedoopt (Du) – baptized.

geheiratet (G) – married.

gehucht (Ne) – hamlet.

gehuwd (Du) – married.

geld – a payment; a tax paid to the crown by landholders under Saxon and Norman kings.

Geld. (Ne) – Gelderland.

gemelli (L) – twin.

gemellus (L) – twin-born; twin.

geminus (L) – twin-born; double; both.

geneal. – genealogy (q.v.).

genealogia (It) (Sp) – pedigree.

genealogy – an account or history of the descent of a person, family or group from an ancestor or ancestors; the study of family pedigrees and the methods of investigation of them, regarded as a science or an art. Abbr. – geneal.

gener (L) – son-in-law; brother-in-law.

generation – a single step or stage in the succession

of natural descent; a rank or remove in genealogy; the average lifetime of man, or the ordinary period of time at which one rank follows another, usually taken to be about 33 years.

genero (L) - to beget; bring to life.

generosi(sus) (L) - of noble birth.

generosos (L) - of noble birth; noble; generous; brave.

geneth (W) - girl.

genetrix (L) - mother.

genialis (L) - pertaining to generation or birth; marry.

genitalis (L) - birth.

genitor (L) - begettor; father.

genitrix (L) - mother.

gens (L) - gentleman (q.v.); the second of a Roman's names.

gent. - gentleman.

gentilis (L) - of the same clan or race.

gentis (L) - gens (q.v.).

gentleman - a man well born; one of a good family though not noble; one entitled to bear a coat of arms; sometimes, anyone above the social condition of a yeoman. (q. v.). Abbr - gent.

gentry - people of good breeding; gentlefolk; in England, those between the nobility and the yeomanry (q.v.).

genus (L) - birth; descent; origin; race; family.

Georgius (L) - George.

Ger. - German, Germany.

Gerardus (L) - Gerard.

germana (L) - sister.

germani (L) - brother.

germanus (L) - (of brothers and sisters), full; genuine, true.

geslachtsboom (Du) - pedigree.

gestorben (G) - died.

gestorven (Du) - died.

gestorven zonder nageslacht (Du) - died without issue.

getauft (G) - baptized.

gf. - *grandfather.

gg. - great grand, (q.v.).

ghost town - an abandoned town.

gift, gifte (D) - married.

gift (No) (Sw) - married.

gigno (L) - to beget; to bear; to be born; to produce.

Gilebertus, Gislebertus (L) - Gilbert.

giorno (It) - day.

giovane, (It) - young.

giovine (It) - young.

giovanetto (It) - boy.

giv. - giving; given.

Glams. (W) - Glamorgan.

Glavorna, Galworna (L) -

Gloucester.

glebe - the cultivable land by a parish church or ecclesiastical benefice; soil.

Glevum (L) - Gloucester.

Glocestria (L) - Gloucester

gloris (L) - sister-in-law.

glos (L) - sister-in-law.

Gloucs. (E) - Gloucester.

Gloucestresc (L) - Gloucestershire.

Gloveceastria, Glovernia (L) - Gloucester.

gm. - *grandmother.

Godefridus (L) - Godfrey.

Godf. - *Godfather.

Godm. - *Godmother.

gods (D) - landed estate.

goodman - householder; husband; an appellation of civility, equivalent to "Mister" or the like, prefixed to the names of persons, as yeomen, under the rank of gentlemen. (see SYA p. 141).

goodwife - the same as goodman for the female sex.

gor hendaid (W) - 2nd great grandfather.

gorss-tante (G) - grandaunt.

gor wyr (W) - great-grandson.

gor wyres (W) - great-granddaughter.

gosse (Sw) - boy.

Goteb9Bohus. (Sw) - Göte-borg & Bohus.

Gotld. (Sw) - Gotland.

gp. - *grandparents.

gr. - grand; great (qq.v.); *grant; *graduate.

G.R. - grave record.

grand - standing in the second or some more remote degree of ancestry or descent; two or more generations removed; generally used in composition, as grandfather, grandson, granduncle, grandniece, etc. Abbr. - g; gr.

grandaevus (L) - of great age, old.

grand mère (Fr) - grandmother.

grand oncle (Fr) - granduncle.

grandonkel (D) - granduncle.

grand-onkel (No) - granduncle.

grand père (Fr) - grandfather.

grandtante (D) - grandaunt.

grand tante (Fr) - grandaunt.

grand-tante (No) - grandaunt.

grant - a general term applicable to all transfers of real property.

Granta, Grantanus Pons (L) - Cambridge.

grantee - one to whom a grant is made.

grantor - a person by whom a grant or conveyance is made.

gravestone inscription -the inscription on a stone laid over or erected near a grave. (for information on customs of the past regarding gravestones see SYA pp. 77-78).

gr/d/o-*granddaughter of.

great - older, younger or more remote by one generation - used before grand to indicate one degree more remote in the direct line of descent; as, great grandfather (a grandfather's or grandmother's father); Abbr.- *g.; gr.; gt. Great great grand father is one more generation removed and may also be written: gg father; second great grandfather. Mother; uncle; aunt, son, daughter, nephew and niece may all be used in combinations as above.

Gregorian Calendar - the calendar now in general use, introduced by Pope Gregory VIII A.D. 1582 and adopted by Great Britain and the English colonies in America in 1752; a reformation of the Julian Calendar. (q. v., also double-dating;

GGr p. 320 ff; SYA pp. 135-38; 1953 HB p. 220).

Grenteburga (L) - Cambridge.

gr. f. - *grandfather.

gr. m. - *grandmother.

Gron. (Ne) - Groningen.

grootmoeder (Du) - grandmother.

grootvader (Du) - grandfather.

gross-, grösser- (G) - great, greater.

grossmutter (G) - grandmother.

gross-onkel (G) - granduncle.

gross-tante (G) - grandaunt.

grossvater (G) - grandfather.

gr/s/o- *grandson of.

g.s. - *gravestone.

gt. - great (q.v.).

Gt. Br. - Great Britain.

gt. gr. - great grand (q.v.).

GTT. - gone to Texas.

gu. - gules (q.v.).

Gualterus (L) - Walter.

guardian - one who has, or is entitled to, the care and management of the person or property, or both, of another, as of a minor or of a person incapable of managing his own affairs.

gudmoder (D) - godmother.

guild - a medieval association of merchants or

craftsmen.

Guillelmus (L) - William.

gules (her) - red.

Gull. (Ic) - Gullbringusysla.

gutshof (Sz) - farm.

gutt (No) - boy.

gweddw, gwraig weddw (W) - widow.

gweddw, gwr gweddw (W) - widower.

gwlad (W) - country.

gwr (W) - husband, man.

gwraig (W) - wife.

H

h. - heir (q.v.); husband.

1/h, 2/h - *first husband, *second husband, etc.

habeas corpus - a writ requiring the body of a person to brought before a judge or court. (L) You shall have the body.

habitator (L) - dweller, inhabitant.

hac (L) - by or this way or side; here; hither.

Hadlev. (D) - Haderslev.

Hainaut. (Bel) - Henegouwen

half aunt - the half sister of a parent.

half brother - a brother by one parent only.

half cousin - the child of half uncle or half aunt.

half uncle - the half brother of a parent.

hameau (Fr) - hamlet.

hamlet - a small group of houses belonging to a parish or village; a little cluster of houses in the country.

Hamps. (E) - Hampshire.

Hann. (G) - Hannover.

Hantonia (L) - Hampshire.

härad (Sw) - local government area.

Haraldus (L) - Harold.

Harefordia (L) - Hereford.

haudattu (Fi) - buried.

Hawisha (L) - Hawise.

hearsay - something heard from another; rumor; report.

hearsay evidence - out-of-court statements, oral or written, when offered as evidence. Not acceptable as evidence under ordinary circumstances.

heb briodi (W) - unmarried.

Heidelbg. (G) - Heidelberg.

heir - one who inherits, or is entitled to succeed to the possession of, any property after the death of its owner; inheritor. Anciently the heir, coheir, heiress or coheiress had the right to transmit arms to their issue, the details of the manner of which have always been regulated by strict rules. The inheritance of land or money does not enter in when considered under the rules of heraldry (q.v.).

heiress - a female heir. (see heir).

Heisa (L) - In Kent.

Helena (L) - Helen.

helmet (Her) - a defensive covering for the head.

hendad (W) - grandfather.

hen daid (W) - great-grand-father.

hen ewythr (W) - grand-uncle.

hen fam (W) - grandmother.

hen fodryb (W) - grand-aunt.

hen nain (W) - great-grand-mother.

Henoforthum (L) - Hereford.

Henricus (L) - Henry.

Heortiforda (L) - Hertford.

Her. - Heraldry.

hera (L) - mistress of a house; lady; dame.

herald - in Great Britain and Ireland, an officer charged with the care of genealogies and armorial bearings (qq.v.); one who publishes or announces; a forerunner. (see Heralds' College).

heraldic - of or pertaining to heralds or heraldry (qq.v.).

heraldic bearing - heraldic symbol or emblazonment.

heraldry - the art or science of a herald (q.v.); the art practice, or science of recording gene-

alogies and blazoning arms, or ensigns armorial. (see SYA pp. 144 146; GGR pp. 217-222; also heir, Heralds' College).

Heralds' College - in England, a corporation, dependent upon the crown, instituted about 1460-85, consisting of Kings-of-arms, Heralds and pursuivants. This retains from the Middle Ages the charge of the armorial bearings of persons privileged to bear them, as well as of the genealogies and kindred subjects. (see heraldry).

heredis (L) - heir.

hereditary societies - associations formed by descendants to honor common ancestors or groups of ancestors, such as Daughters of the American Revolution, First Families of Virginia, etc.

hereditas (L) - heirship; inheritance.

Hereffordscr' (L) - Herefordshire.

Herefs. (E) - Hereford.

hermana (Sp) - sister.

hermano (Sp) - brother.

herred (D) - division or district within a county.

hers. - *herself.

Hertfordia (L) - Hertford.

Herts. (E) – Hertford.

herus (L) – master of the house or family; lord; owner.

Hess/N (G) – Hessen Nassau.

HG. – High German.

hic (L) – here; in this matter.

hic jocet sepultus (L) – here lies buried. Abbr. – H.J.S.

hic requiescit in pace (L) – here rests in peace. Abbr. – H.R.I.P.

hic sepultus (L) – hic situs (q.v.).

hic situs (L) – here is buried. Abbr. – h.s.

hide of land – a measure of land common in Domesday Book and in old English charters varying from 80 to 120 acres.

Hieremias (L) – Jeremiah.

Hieronymus (L) – Jerome.

hiippakunta (Fi) – bishopric or diocese.

hija (Sp) – daughter.

hija natural (Sp) – natural or illegitimate daughter.

hija politica (Sp) – daughter-in-law.

hijo (Sp) – son.

hijo natural (Sp) – illegitimate son.

hijo politico (Sp) – son-in-law.

hinter (D) – posterior.

hist. – history, historian.

historical method or form – the mode or system used by writers and teachers (genealogists) basing their work and teachings upon the facts shown by historical research and the inductions to be drawn from them. (see legal method).

hims. – *himself.

Hjorrg. (D) – Hjørring.

H.J.S. – hic jocet sepultus (q.v.).

H.M. – His or Her Majesty.

h.m. – hoc mense (q.v.).

Hnapp. (Ic) – Hnappadalssysla.

hoc loco (L) – in this place.

hoc mense (L) – in this month. Abbr. – h.m.

hoc tempore (L) – at this time. Abbr. – h.t.

Hohenz. (G) – Hohenzollern.

Holbaek (G) – Holbaek.

Holland Dutch – immigrants from The Netherlands who settled in the U.S. (Not Pennsylvania Dutch q.v.).

holographic (Law) – of wills, totally in the handwriting of the testator (witnesses not required).

homage – the act whereby the vassal gave fealty to his lord.

hombre (Sp) – man.

homestead application – the application filed under

the Homestead Act authorizing the sale of public lands, in parcels of 160 acres to each settler. (see ABC p. 75).

homme (Fr) – man.

homo (L) – man.

hon. – *honor; honorary; honorable (q.v.).

honorable – a title of distinction given to certain off.cials and others, usually simply as a courtsey title. Abbr. – hon.

hora (L) – hour; season (of the year); time.

Hordald. (No) – Hordaland.

hrepp (Ic) – rural municipality or division of county.

H.R.I.P. – hic requiescit in pace (q.v.).

h.s. – hic situs (q.v.).

h.t. – hoc tempore (q.v.).

Hte Garonne (Fr) – Haute Garonne.

Hte Loire (Fr) – Haute Loire.

Hte Marne (Fr) – Haute Marne.

Hte Saone (Fr) – Haute Saone.

Htes Alpes (Fr) – Hautes Alpes.

Hte Savoie (Fr) – Haute Savoie.

Htes Pyr. (Fr) – Hautes Pyénees.

Hte Vienne (Fr) – Haute Vienne.

Ht Rhin. (Fr) – Haut Rhin.

Hugo (L) – Hugh.

Huguenot – a French Protestant in the 16th and 17th centuries; one of the members of the Reformed or Calvinistic communion who was driven by the thousands into exile in England, Holland, Germany and America.

hujus (L) – his; this.

hujus mense (L) – this month's.

Humfredus (L) – Humfrey.

hund. – hundred (q.v.).

hundred – in England, later also in Ireland, a division of a county, formerly having its own local court (the hundred court or moot); also, the body of land holders and residents of the hundred; in U.S., derived from the Eng. hundred, formerly existed in Virginia, Maryland, and Pennsylvania and still survives in Delaware. Abbr. – hund; originally an area sufficient to support 100 families.

Huntedon (L) – Huntingdonshire.

Huntindonia, Huntundona (L) – Huntingdon.

Hunts. (E) – Huntingdon.

husbandman – a master of

the household; a farmer. Abbr. - *husbn.

husbandry - farming; the various branches of agriculture.

husbn. - *husbandman (q.v.).

husbonde (D) - husband.

husmand (D) - small farmer owning own house.

hustru (D) (No) (Sw) - wife.

hynaf (W) - eldest.

hynafiad (W) - ancestor.

I

i - sometimes interchanged with j in Old English.

I. - *inventory (q.v.).

iacet hic (L) - here lies. Abbr. - i.h.

iäkäs (Fi) - aged, old.

ib.; ibid. - ibidem (q.v.).

ibidem (L) - in the same place; the same book, chapter, page, etc. Abbr. - ib.; ibid.

idem (L) - the same.

idem quod (L) - the same as. Abbr. - i.q.

id est (L) - that is. Abbr. - i.e.

I.D.N. - In Dei Nomie - in the Name of God.

i.e. - id est (q.v.).

I. et L. (Fr) - Indre et Loire.

I. et V. (Fr) - Ille et Vilaine.

ieuaf, ieuengaf (W) - youngest.

i.f. - ipse fecit (q.v.).

ign. - *ignorant; ignotus (q.v.).

ignotus (L) - unknown; low born.

i.h. - iacet hic (q.v.).

ikä (Fi) - age.

ikäinen (Fi) - aged.

il.; i-l. - *in-law (q.v.).

Ill. - Illinois.

ille (L) - he; she; it; that one, the aforesaid; the very same.

illégitime (Fr) - illegitimate.

illegittimo (It) - illegitimate.

im alter von (G) - aged.

immigrant - one who immigrates; one who comes to a country for the purpose of permanent residence; the correlative of emigrant (q.v.).

imprimis (L) - in the first place; chiefly; especially.

inc - incomplete.

incl. - included, inclusive.

incognitus (L) - unknown.

incola (L) - an inhabitant.

incompertus (L) - unknown.

incumbent - the holder of an office or ecclesiastical benefice; the rector, vicar or curate in charge of an English parish.

Ind. - Indiana; *Indians.

inde (L) - thence; from that place; from that time.

indenture- a mutual agreement between two or more parties, whereof each party has usually a counterpart or duplicate; a contract by which an apprentice is bound to a master; a formal or official document, as a certificate or an inventory (originally one prepared in duplicate).

Ind. T.; Ind. Ter. - Indian Territory.

indidem (L) - from the same place or thing.

ined. - ineditus (q.v.).

ineditus (L) - not made known; unpublished. Abbr. - ined.

inf. - *infant; *informed.

infans (L) - childish; speechless; muted; little child.

infans cui quis in baptismo sponsor exstitit (L) - godchild.

infante (It) - infant.

info. - *information.

infra (L) - under; below.

inh. - *inherited.

inhab. - *inhabitant.

inheritance - the acquisition of property, real or personal by one person as heir to another; that which is or may be inherited.

inheritor - heir; he that inherits. (see inheritance).

inhibition - restraint; prohibition; a writ from a higher court staying an inferior judge from further proceedings in a specific case.

in-law - a relative by marriage. (cousin -in-law, son-in-law, relative-in-law, (qq.v.). Abbr. - *il; *-l.

in loc. cit; - in loco citato (q.v.).

in loco citato (L) - in the place cited. Abbr. - in loc. cit.

in mem. - in memoriam (q. v.).

in memoriam (L) - in memory of. Abbr. - in mem.

innubus (L) - unmarried.

innupta (L) - unmarried.

inq. - *inquiry.

inquilinus (L) - of foreign birth; inmate; lodger.

inquisitiones post mortem- Inquiries made by the Crown on the death of an estate owner as to the sums due prior to inheritance by heir.

ins. - *insert.

institus (L) - inborn; natural adopted.

int. - *intentions.

int. - interested.

inter (L) -between; among; in comparison.

intermarriage -reciprocal marriage, as between two

families tribes or casts; consanguineous marriage; in breeding.

intestate - dying without having made a will (he died intestate).

intestatus (L) - intestate.

inuptus, inupta (L) - unmarried.

inv. - *inventory (q.v.).

inventory - an account, catalogue, or schedule, made by an executor or administrator, of all the goods and chattels, and sometimes of the real estate, of a deceased person. Abbr. - *I.; *inv.; invt.

Invern. (Sc) - Inverness.

invt. - inventory (q.v.).

I. of Man (E) - Isle of Man.

I. of Wight (E) - Isle of Wight.

ipse fecit (L) - he did it himself. Abbr. - i.f.

ipso facto (L) - by the act itself.

i.q. - idem quod (q.v.).

Ir. - Irish, Ireland.

Ire. - Ireland.

isä (Fi) - father.

Isabella (L) - Isabel, Elizabeth.

isänsetä (Fi) - granduncle.

isäntäti (Fi) - grandaunt.

Isiacum (L) - Oxford.

Isidis Vadum (L) - Oxford.

isoäidiñäti (Fi) - great-grandmother.

isoäti (Fi) - grandmother.

isoisä (Fi) - grandfather.

isoisänisä (Fi) - great-grandfather.

isoisänisän isoisänisä (Fi) - 4th great-grandfather.

isoisän isoisä (Fi) - 2nd great-grandfather.

isoisän isoisänisä (Fi) - 3rd great-grandfather.

issue - progeny; a child or children; offspring.

Isuria (L) - Yorkshire.

Isurovicum (L) - York.

It. - Italy or Italian.

iunioris (L) - juvenis (q.v.) (see also "J").

J

j - sometimes interchanged with "i" in Old English (iij=3, Roman Numeral).

jaar (Du) - year.

Jacobus (L) - James, Jacob.

jahr (G) - year.

Jälkisäädos (Fi) - will, testament.

Jamtld. (Sw) - Jämtland.

Johanna (L) - Joan, Jane.

Johannes (L) - John.

jointure - a joint tenancy of an estate, or the estate so held; an estate settled on a wife to be taken by her in lieu of dower.

jongen (Du) - boy.

jongste (Du) - youngest.

Jonkpg. (Sw) - Jönköping.

jour (Fr) – day.

jour. – journal (q.v.).

journal – a diary; an account of daily transactions and events; a record of transactions kept by a deliberate body or assembly. Abbr. – jour.

joven (Sp) – young.

JP. – Justice of Peace.

Jr. – junior (q.v.).

juba (L) – crest (of a helmet) (see coat-of-arms).

jud.; *judic. – judicial; *judicious.

juengster, juengst (G) – youngest.

jugo (L) – to marry; to join.

Julian Calendar – the calendar introduced by Julius Ceasar in 46 B.C. and replaced by the Gregorian Calendar (q.v.) 1582 A.D.

jun. – junior (q.v.).

junior (L) – younger. During the Middle Ages and later the terms Jr. and Sr. applied only until the eldest died, then Jr. might change to Sr. if he also had a son with the same name. Thus, he might be Jr. the fore part of his life and Sr. the latter. Abbr. Jr.; jun.; junr.

junr. – junior (q.v.).

juv. – juvenis (q.v.).

juvenalis (L) – youthful.

juvenca (L) – young cow; girl.

juvencus (L) – young bullock; young man.

juvenilis (L) – youthful.

juvenis (L) – young. Abbr.– juv.

K

k. – *killed; king.

Kanc', Kantia (L) – Kent.

Kans. – Kansas.

kantaisä (Fi) – progenitor.

kanton (Sz) – state. (canton)

Käräjäkunta (Fi). – subdivision of a judicial district.

Karlegion (L) – Chester.

Karlsr. (G) – Karlsruhe.

kastettu (Fi) – baptized.

kauppala (Fi) – smaller city.

kaupunki (Fi) – city.

kerk (Du) – church parish.

Kihlakunta (Fi) – local government area.

Kincard. (Sc) – Kincardine.

kind (Du) (G) – child.

kindred – belonging to the same family or race; related.

king-of-arms – the chief heraldic officer of a country. (see heraldry; Heralds' College).

kirchen-gemeinde (G) – church parish.

kirk (Scot) – church.

Kirkby's Inquest – a survey

of the English county of York taken by John de Kirby 1284-5 A.D. (see GGR p. 229).

Kirkcubd. (Sc) - Kirkcudbright.

kirkjustadur (Ic) - church place.

Kjos. (Ic) - Kjosarsysla.

klein (G) - little.

kleindochter (Du) - granddaughter.

kleinkind (G) - infant.

kleinzoon (Du) - grandson.

kn. - *known.

knabe (G) - boy.

knight - a military attendant, servant, or follower; in feudal times a mounted man-at-arms serving a king or other superior, commonly in return for a tenure of land, especially, one, generally of noble birth, who, after serving regularly as a page and squire was admitted to a special military rank; in modern times, a man upon whom a corresponding dignity has been conferred by a sovereign in recognition of personal merit. Abbr. - knt.

knight bachelor - a knight of the most ancient, but lowest, order of English knights, and not a member of any order of chivalry.

knt. - knight (q.v.).

kommune (D) - a municipality.

kone (D) - wife.

Konstz. (G) - Konstanz.

kontrakt (Sw) - rural deanery containing a number of rectoral districts.

köping (Sw) - commercial center without a city charter.

Koppbg. (Sw) - Kopparberg.

Kreis (G) - county.

Krnstad. (Sw) - Kristianstad

Kronobg. (Sw) - Kronoberg.

Kt. - knight.

kusin (Sw) - cousin.

kusine (D) (No) - female cousin.

kuollut (Fi) - died.

kuollut jättämättä rintaperillistä (Fi) - died without issue.

kuukausi (Fi) - month.

kvinde (D) - woman.

kvinna (Sw) - woman.

kvinne (No) - woman.

Ky. - Kentucky.

kylä (Fi) - village.

kyrke byn (No) - sub-division of a parish.

L

l. - liber (q.v.).

L.; *(L) - Latin (q.v.).

La. - Louisiana.

lääni (Fi) - county.

labr. - *laborer.

Laetitia (L) - Lettice.

lamina - a thin plate. The acetate foil welded to both sides of a document, after sterilization, to help preserve it.

laminate - Cover with laminae (q.v.).

län (Sw) - county.

Lancastra (L) - Lancashire

Lancastria (L) - Lancaster.

Lancs. (E) - Lancashire.

land (D) (Du) (G) (No) (Sw)- country.

land application - a formal request for rights in, or eventual title to public lands.

Land Entry Papers - documents filed in connections with entry on public land. (see ABC p. 74).

landgemeinde (G) - village, rural municipality.

land grant - a grant of land by the government, esp. for roads or railroads, or for agricultural or industrial colleges.

Landinium (L) - London.

land records - various records which have been made regarding the transfer of land from the government to individuals and from person to person. (see ABC p. 74; GGR p. 81).

landsby (D) - village.

landskap (Sw) - older name for län, but with different bounds.

langen (G) - long.

Lania (L) - Lancashire.

lanius (L) - butcher.

lapseton (Fi) - childless.

lapsi (Fi) - child.

Lat. - Latin (q.v.).

Latin - the language of ancient Latium and of Rome and until modern times the dominant language of school, church and state in western Europe. Because of its widespread use in recording genealogical data, we present this index with many of the more common terms and their translations to assist you when searching the older records. Abbr. - L.; *(L); Lat.

Laurentius (L) - Lawrence.

L.C. - Library of Congress.

ld. - *land.

L.D.S. - Church of Jesus Christ of Latter-Day Saints (Mormon).

leeftijd (Du) - age.

Legacestra (L) - Chester.

Legacestria, Legecestria (L) - Leicester.

legacy - something coming from an ancestor or predecessor; a gift of property by will, esp. money or other personal property.

legal description - the description of a particular parcel of land, according to the official plat of survey.

legal method–documentary method of recording history or genealogy. Each and every step or point is established by original, certified or photostat copies, acceptable in court. (see historical method).

legate – an ambassador or envoy; a delegate or messenger; under Roman History a governor or assistant to the governor of a province.

legatee – one to whom a legacy is bequeathed.

Legio VI Victrix (L) – York.

Legio XX Victrix (L) – Chester.

Legionum Urbs (L) – Chester.

Legoria (L) – Leicester.

Leicestresc' (L) – Leicestershire.

Lecestria, Leogereceastria, Legrecastrum, Licestria, Ligeria, Ligrecastrum, Legoria (L) – Leicester.

Leics. (E) – Leicester.

leskimies (Fi) – widower.

L.'et C. (Fr) – Loiret Cher.

L.'et G. (Fr) – Lotet Garonne.

letter of attorney – see power of attorney.

letters of administration – the instrument by which an administrator or administratrix is authorized to administer the goods or estate of a deceased person.

letters testamentary – an instrument issued by a court or public official authorizing an executor to take control of and dispose of the estate of a decedent.

letzter wille (G) – last will, testament.

li. – *lived; *living.

lib. – liber (q.v.); library.

liber (L) – book; free spoken; wine. Abbr. – l.; lib.

Liberate Rolls – Orders to English royal treasurers to pay monies as specified.

liberi (L) – children; grandchildren.

liberty (E) – a special division of a parish or town.

lic. – *license.

Lidocollina (L) – Lincoln.

Lieg. (Bel) – Luik.

liege – a liege lord; a feudal superior to whom allegiance and service are due; a liege subject; a vassal bound to feudal service and allegiance;

a liege man.

Lieut. – Lieutenant.

Lincolnia, Lincolinum (L)– Lincoln.

Lincolnscr' (L) – Lincoln-shire.

Lincs. (E) – Lincoln.

Lindecolina, Lindecolli-num, Lindocollinum (L)– Lincoln.

Lindonium (L) – London.

Lindum, Lindum Colonia (L) – Lincoln.

lineage – ancestry or ex-traction (See lineal).

lineal – consisting of, or being in, a direct line of ancestry or descendants; descended in a direct line; in the line of suc-cession through lineage. Collateral relationship is not "lineal" though the expression "collateral lines" is not uncommon.

Lippe Det. (G) – Lippe Detmold.

liv. – *living; *lived.

liv. abt. – *lived about.

l.l. – loco ladato (q.v.).

ll. – lines.

lnd – land.

locale – a place or locality.

locality file – the geograph-ical catalogue of a gene-alogical library.

loc. cit. – loco citato (q.v.).

loco (L) – to place; to lay; to let for hire; to farm out.

loco citato (L) – in the place cited. Abbr. – loc. cit.

loco laudato (L) – in the place cited. Abbr. – l.l.

locus (L) – place; position; rank; place of the seal.

Loer. (G) – Loerrach.

Loire Inf (Fr) – Loire In-férieure.

Loncastria (L) – Lancaster.

Lond. (E) – London.

Londinia, Londinium, Lon-dinium Augusta, Lond-inum, Londonia (L) – London.

longeavus (L) – of great age; ancient.

Longfd. (Ire) – Longford.

loyalist – in the American Rev., one opposed to sep-aration from Great Brit-ain. (see ABC p. 71).

l.s. – locus sigilli (q.v.).

Lucas (L) – Luke.

Lucia (L) – Lucy.

ludimagister (L) – school-master.

Lundinium, Lundonia (L) – London.

Lunia (L) – Lancashire.

Lux. (Bel) – Luxemburg.

M

M.; m. – man; maritus (q.v.); married.

m/1, m/2 – *married first, *married second, etc.

maa (Fi) – country.

maakunta (Fi) – older name for lääni, but with different bounds.

maand (Du) – month.

maaned (D) – month.

maatila (Fi) – farm.

mab, map (W) – son, son of.

Mabilia, Mabilla (L) – Mabel.

Mac, (prefix) – Scotch Gaelic and Irish signifying son.

madre (It) (Sp) – mother.

maedchen (G) – girl, maiden.

mag – magistrate.

maggiornato (It) – eldest, firstborn.

magna (L) – great.

Magna Charta; Magna Carta – the Great Charter to which the English barons forced King John to affix his seal June 15, 1215; a constitution guaranteeing rights and privileges.

maiden name – the name of a woman prior to marriage.

Maior (L) – Mayor.

Maj. – Major.

major natu (L) – (in date) prior.

Major – Mayor.

majores (L) – ancestors.

majoris (L) – greater; older.

mak. – *making.

maka (Sw) – wife.

make (Sw) – husband.

Malmhs. (Sw) – Malmöhus.

mam (W) – mother.

man (Du) (Sw) – husband, man.

Man. (Can) – Manitoba.

månad (Sw) – month.

mand (D) – husband, man.

måned (No) – month.

mann (G) – man.

mann (No) – husband, man.

Mannh. (G) – Mannheim.

manor –house against which geld (q.v.) was charged; hence, the land represented in the house, or any plot of land treated as a unit for that purpose; a landed estate or territorial unit, orig. of the nature of a feudal lordship; the mansion of a lord and the land pertaining to it.

manuscript – a composition written with the hand, as an ancient book, document, etc., or an unprinted modern book, piece of music, etc. Abbr. – ms.; MS.; plural Mss.; mss.

map (W) – son of.

Margareta (L) – Margaret.

Margeria (L) – Margery.

mari (Fr) – husband.

Maria (L) – Mary.

marido (Sp) – husband.

marié, mariée (Fr) – married.

marita (L) – married woman; wife.

maritato (It) - married.

marito (It) - husband.

maritus (L) - bridegroom; (of man) married. Abbr. - M.

marriage bond - a financial guarantee that no impediment to the marriage existed. Furnished by the intended bridegroom or by his friends.

marriage by contract or marriage of convenience - a marriage contracted, rather for the advantage arising out of it, such as keeping an estate in a family, acquiring social position, etc.

marriage license - a written authorization granted by a qualified governmental official to a (named) man and woman to marry.

marriage out of unity - a marriage contrary to the Friends (q.v.) order. Also referred to as "marriage by a priest." "outgoing marriage", marriage out of meeting".

Marta (L) - Martha.

marwodd (W) - died.

marwodd yn ddiepil (W) - died without issue.

Mass. - Massachusetts.

mater (L) - mother; matron; maternal love, etc.

materta magna (L) - grandmother's sister (grandaunt).

matertera (L) - mother's sister; aunt.

matertera magna (L) - grandmother's sister (grandaunt).

matrimonium (L) - matrimony. Abbr. - mm.

Mattaeus (L) - Matthew.

maximus natu (L) - eldest; first born.

Mayflower Compact - an agreement, constituting the first written American constitution, signed by 41 of the Pilgrim Fathers in the cabin of the ''Mayflower'' Nov. 21, 1620, to serve as a form of government, because the Pilgrims possessed no charter. Many ancestral lines run back to and beyond these Pilgrim Fathers (q.v.). (see 1953 HB p. 220; Puritan).

m. bn. - *marriage banns (see banns).

Md. - Maryland.

md. -*married.

MD. - Middle Dutch.

Me. - Maine.

media (L) - middle.

medicus (L) - physician.

meisje (Du) - girl.

Melamon (L) - In Devonshire.

Melezo (L) - In Dorsetshire.

mem. - *membership;

member; memorials; memoir.

memorial - anything intended to preserve the memory of a person or event; a record of memoir; a note; an abstract.

mensis (L) - month.

ment. - *mentioned.

merch (W) - daughter.

Mercia (L) - Mercy.

mère (Fr) - mother.

Merions. (W) - Merioneth.

mes (Sp) - month.

mese (It) - month.

Messrs. - plural of mister (q.v.).

M.et L. (Fr) - Maine-et-Loire.

M.et M. (Fr) - Meurthe-et-Moselle.

MHG. - Middle High German.

M.I. - monumental inscription.

mi. - miles, mile.

Mich. - Michigan.

Michaelis (L) - Michael.

microfilm - a strip of photographic film, often of standard motion-picture film size, used for making photographic record on reduced scale of printed matter, manuscripts, etc., as for storage or transmission in small space, which is enlarged for reading. Used extensively for copying genealogical records of all kinds.

Middle English - the English language of the period A.D. 1100-1500.

Middlesexa (L) - Middlesex

Middlesexia (L) - Middlesex.

Middx. (E) - Middlesex.

mies (Fi) - man, husband.

m-i-l. - *mother-in-law.

miles (L) - knight; soldier.

Milidunum (L) - In Devonshire.

milit. - *military.

militi(a)(s) (L) - miles; military service.

min. - minister; minor; minutes.

minima natu (L) - youngest.

minimus natu (L) - youngest.

Minn. - Minnesota.

minoris (L) - lesser; younger.

minority - state or period of being under age or a minor.

mis (W) - month.

Miss. - Mississippi.

Mister - in early times, a title of respect given only to those who held important civil office or were of gentle blood. If a man did not act in accordance with the dignity of the title it was taken away from him. (see SYA p. 141). Abbr. - Mr.

Mistress - in the 17th and 18th centuries the title "Mistress" was one of social distinction as a general rule and did not necessarily mean that the woman to whom applied was or had been married. Sometimes it meant widowhood. Abbr. - Mrs. (see SYA p. 141).

mittel (G) - middle.

Mittelfr. (G) - Mittelfranken.

MLG. - Middle Low German.

Mlle. - Mademoiselle.

M. Lothian (Sc) - Midlothian

MM - *Monthly Meeting (q.v.); Messieurs.

mm. - matrimonium (q.v.).

Mme. - Madam.

Mo. - Missouri.

mo. - month; *mother.

moder (D) (Sw) - mother.

modryb (W) - aunt.

moeder (Du) - mother.

moglie (It) - wife.

moiety - about a half; part.

mois (Fr) - month.

Monagn. (Ir) - Monaghan.

monat (G) - month.

Monms. (E) (W) - Monmouth

Monmuthsc', Monovaga, Monumethia (L) - Monmouth.

Mons. - Monsignor.

Mont. - Montana.

Montg. (W) - *Montgomery.

Monthly Meeting - the Society of Friends (q.v.) is regulated by periodic meetings known as Meetings for Business. One or more congregations comprise a Monthly Meeting, held once a month; one or more Monthly Meetings form a Quarterly Meeting, held once in three months; the Quarterly Meetings within a stated geographical area form a Yearly Meeting, called a Society of Friends. Many records are preserved of these meetings giving much genealogical information. The records kept in Monthly Meetings consist of birth, marriage and death, also minutes or proceedings, discussions, condemnations and disownments. Two sets of meetings were kept, one for male and one for female members. (see marriage out of unity). Abbr. - *MM.

mor (D) (No) - mother.

mor. - *mother.

morbroder (D) - mother's brother (uncle).

morbror (Sw) - mother's brother (uncle).

More og R. (No) - More og Romsdal.

morfar (D) (No) (Sw) -

mother's father (grand-father).

morfars far (Sw) – mother's father's father (great-grandfather).

morfars mor (Sw) – mother's father's mother (great-grandmother).

mormor (D) (No) (Sw) – mother's mother (grandmother).

mormors far (Sw) – mother's mother's father (great-grandfather).

mormors mor (Sw) – mother's mother's mother (great-grandmother).

mors (L) – death; corpse.

mors farbror (Sw) – mother's father's brother (granduncle).

mors faster (Sw) – mother's father's sister (grandaunt).

mors morbror (Sw) – mother's mother's brother (granduncle).

mors moster (Sw) – mother's mother's sister (grandaunt).

mort, morte (Fr) – died.

mortality schedules – taken by census enumerators in 1850, 1860, 1870 and 1880 they give information as to all persons dying within the twelve months preceeding the taking of the census. They are filed in Washington, D.C. (see ABC p. 117).

morte sua defungi (L) – to die natural death.

mortis (L) – death; corpse.

morto (It) – died.

morto senza prole (It) – died without issue.

moster (D) (Sw) – mother's sister (aunt).

mother – female parent; in early times "mother" might mean mother-in-law, stepmother, or even one not of blood or marital relationship; a title of endearment. (see SYA p. 140).

mother-in-law – the mother of one's husband or wife; a stepmother (not in standard use at present).

movable feast days – see feast days.

Moyses (L) – Moses.

Mr. – Mister (q.v.).

Mrs. – Mistress (q.v.).

Ms.; ms. – manuscript (q.v.).

Mss.; mss. – manuscripts.

mtg. – meeting (see monthly Meeting); mortgage.

muchacha (Sp) – girl.

muchacho (Sp) – boy.

mujer (Sp) – woman, wife.

municipalsamhälle (Sw) – municipality, community with some local jurisdictions.

muniment chest or room – repository of records of a family usually relating to property or land; also other papers.

muriő (Sp) - died.

Murionio (L) - in Dorsetshire.

muriő sin hijos (Sp) - died without children.

muriő sin sucesión (Sp) - died without issue.

mutter (G) - mother.

my/d - *my daughter.

Myr. (Ic) - Myrasysla.

mythology - the collective myths describing the gods of a people, esp., demigods and legendary human beings in stories which involve supernatural elements; the science which treats of myths.

N

n. -natus; *nephew; nomen; north; northern; *nupta (qq.v.); name.

N.A. - National Archives.

nacido, nacio (Sp) - born.

nactus (L) - born.

nai (W) - nephew.

naimaton (Fi) -unmarried.

nain (W) - grandmother.

nainen (Fi) - woman.

naitu (Fi) - married.

nam - *named.

Namur (Bel) - Namen.

nata (L) - daughter.

nat. - *natus (q.v.).

nato (It) - born.

natural son or daughter - actually begotten by one (opp. to adopted), esp., in wedlock; it also means born out of wedlock or illegitimate; consanguineous; Native-born.

naturel, naturelle (Fr) - illegitimate.

natus (L) - birth; age; son; offspring. Abbr. - n.; *nat.

N.B. (E) - North Britain.

N.B. (Can) -New Brunswick

N. bottn. (Sw) -Norrbotten.

N.C. - North Carolina.

n.d. - no date.

N. Dak. - North Dakota.

N.E. - New England.

ne. - northeast.

Nebr. - Nebraska.

né, née (Fr) - born.

necrology - an obituary notice or a list of persons who have died within a certain time.

nee - born (placed after the name of a married woman to introduce her maiden name) (Mrs. Jones, nee Smith).

neer (Du) - male cousin.

neefje (Du) - nephew.

neefe (G) - nephew.

N.E.H. & G.R., - New England Historic & Genealogical Register.

nephew - a son of one's brother or sister; a son of one's husband's or wife's brother or sister; (in euphemistic use) an illegitimate son of an ecclesiastic; a grandson; a male descendant of more remote degree. Abbr. – *n.

nephew-in-law – husband of one's niece. Abbr. – *neph-i-l.

neph-i-l – *nephew-in-law (q. v.).

nepos (L) – grandson; nephew.

nepotis (L) – grandson; nephew; descendant.

neptis (L) – granddaughter.

Neth. – Netherlands.

neu (G) – new.

Nev. – Nevada.

neveu (Fr) – nephew.

nevø (D) (No) – nephew.

new style calendar – see Gregorian calendar; double dating.

nfi. – no further information.

nfk. – nothing further known.

Nfld. – Newfoundland including Labrador.

N.H. – New Hampshire.

N. Ire. – Northern Ireland.

nicht (Du) – female cousin.

nichte (G) – niece.

nichtie (Du) – niece.

nickname – a name added to or substituted for the proper name of a person, place, etc. a familiar form of a proper name, as Jim for James.

Nicolaus (L) – Nicholas.

Nicole (L) – Lincoln.

niece – the daughter of a brother or sister.

Niederb. (G) – Niederbayern

niese (No) – niece.

nieta (Sp) – granddaughter.

nieto (Sp) – grandson.

niña (Sp) – small girl.

niña pequeña (Sp) – infant girl.

niño (Sp) – small boy.

niño pequeño (Sp) – infant boy.

nipote (f) (It) – niece.

nipote (m) (It) – nephew.

nipotina (It) – granddaughter.

nipotino (It) – grandson.

N. Isf. (Ic) – Nordur-Isafjardarsysla.

nith (W) – niece.

N.J. – New Jersey.

N. Mex. – New Mexico.

N. Mul. (Ic) – Nordur-Mulasysla.

nm. – *name.

nmed. – *was named.

nms. – *names.

nw. – northwest.

nobilitas (L) – high birth; renown.

No. Brab. (Ne) – North Brabant.

N. Oestr. (Aus) – Niederoesterreich.

No. Holl. (Ne) – North Holland.

noin (Fi) – about.

nomen (L) – name; family;

Abbr. - n.

non (L) - not.

Non–Conformist - one who refuses to conform to an established church or the Church of England.

Nor. - Norway, Norwegian.

Nordhumbra, Nordhumbria (L) - Northumberland.

Nordld. (No) - Nordland.

Nordovolca, Norfolcia (L)- Norfolk.

Norf. (E) - Norfolk.

Norffolca (L) - Norfolk.

Norfolca (L) - Norfolk.

Northamptonia, Northantuna (L) - Northampton.

Northanimbria (L) - Northumberland.

Northantescr' (L) - Northamptonshire.

Northantonia (L) - Northampton.

Northants. (E) -Northampton.

Northimbria (L) - Northumberland.

Northum. (E) - Northumberland.

Northumbria, Northymbria (L) - Northumberland.

Northumberlanda (L) - Northumberland.

not. - *noted.

nothis (L) - spurious; illegitimate.

nothus (L) - spurious, illegitimate.

Notingehamsc', Nottingamia (L) - Nottingham.

Notts. (E) - Nottingham.

nova nupta (L) - bride.

noverca (L) - stepmother.

novus (L) - new; young; fresh.

novus maritus (L) - bridegroom.

n.p. or d. - no place or date.

nr. - near.

N.S. (Can) - Nova Scotia.

N.S. - New Style (of dating since 1752) (see double dating; Julian calendar).

N. Thing. (Ic) - Nordur Thingeviarsysla.

N. Tronglg. (No) - Nord Trøndelag.

nubo (L) - to marry (a husband).

nuncupative - (of wills, etc) oral rather than written; given before witnesses.

nuorin (Fi) - youngest.

nupital - of or pertaining to marriage or the marriage ceremony.

nupta (L) - (of a woman) married. Abbr. - *n.

nuptiae (L) - marriage.

nuptialis (L) - nupital (q.v.).

nuptus (L) - married.

nurus (L) - daughter-in-law; young woman.

N.W. Terr. (Can) - Northwest Territories.

N.X.N. - * no christian name.

N.Y. - New York.

N.Y.G. & B.R. - New York

Genealogical and Biographical Record.

N.Z. - New Zealand.

O

o. - *oath; optimus (q.v.).

O' - a prefix to ancient Irish family names followed by the genitive case of the name of the ancestor, as O'Neil (nom. Niall). Before surnames of females, O' is replaced in Irish by ni, daughter. It prefixes H before a vowel, as Oh Airt, O'Hart. The apostrophe is due to the mistaken idea that O stands for of.

oäkta (Sw) - illegitimate.

OB - *Order Book.

ob. - obiit; obiter (qq.v.).

ob. caelebs (L) - died unmarried.

ober (G) - upper.

Oberb. (G) - Oberbavern.

Oberfr. (G) - Oberfranken.

obiit (L) - he or she died. Abbr. - ob.; obt.

obiit sine prole (L) - he or she died without issue. (childless). Abbr. - ob.s.p.

obiit sine prole masculus (L) - he or she died without male issue. Abbr. - *ob.s.p.m.

obiit vita patris (L) - died in the lifetime of his or her father. Abbr. - *ob. v.p.

obiter (L) - incidently. Abbr. - ob.

obituary - pertaining to or recording a death.

ob.s.p. - obiit sine prole (q.v.).

ob.s.p.m. -*obiit sine prole masculus (q.v.).

obt. - obiit (q.v.).

ob. unm. - *he or she died unmarried.

ob.v.p. - *obiit vita patris (q.v.).

o.c. - only child; opere citato (q.v.).

Occidua Wallia (L) - Cornwall.

OE.; O.E. - Old English (q.v.).

oed (W) - age, aged.

off.; *offi. - official.

Offenbg. (G) - Offenburg.

O. F. S. - Orange Free State (So. Africa).

oft. - *often.

ogift (Sw) - unmarried.

O. Gotld. (Sw) - Östergötland.

O. Ijsel. (Ne) - Overijssel (Overyssel).

Okla. - Oklahoma.

Olaus (L) - Olaf, Olave.

oldebarn (D) - great-grandchild.

oldefader (D) - great-grandfather.

oldefar (No) - great-grandfather.

oldemoder (D) - great-grandmother.

oldemor (No) - great-grand-mother.

Oldenbg. (G) - Oldenburg.

Old English - the English of periods before 1100; Anglo-Saxon; the form of black letters used by English printers from the 15th to the 18th century. Abbr. - OE.; O.E.

old style calender - see Julian calendar, double-dating. Abbr. - O.S.; o/s.

omkring (No) (Sw) - about.

omstreeks (Du) - about.

oncle (Fr) - uncle.

onecht (Du) - illegitimate.

ongehuwd (Du) - unmarried.

onkel (D) (G) (No) - uncle.

Ont. - Ontario.

O. Oestr. (Aus) - Ober-oesterreich.

oom (Du) - uncle.

o.p. - out of print.

op. cit. - opere citato (q.v.).

operarius (L) - laborer.

opere citato (L) - in the work cited. Abbr. - o.c.; op. cit.

Opfalz. (G) - Oberpfalz.

oppeto (L) - to go to meet; to perish; to die.

oppidanus (L) - of or in a town (other than Rome).

optimas (L) - aristocrat.

optimus (L) - the best. Abbr. - o.

or. (Her) - yellow or gold color.

orbitas (L) - orphanage; widowhood.

orbo (L) - to bereave (of parents, children, etc.).

orbus (L) - bereaved, childless; parentless.

ord. - ordained; ordinance; ordinary (court).

Oreg. - Oregon.

org. - organization.

orig. - origin; original.

origo (L) - beginning; birth; origin.

oriundus (L) - descended; sprung from.

Orkney. (Sc) - Orkney Islands.

orphan - a child bereaved by the death of both parents, or, less commonly, of one parent.

orphan chamber - the chamber or court having jurisdiction over minors, wills, etc., and presided over by the orphan master.

orphan's court - in the U.S. and other countries orphans have been recognized as wards of the state and governmental provision is made for their care through the orphan's courts. The duty of the state to provide for orphans was first recognized in the early part of the 17th century.

ort (G) – place.

ortus (L) – rising; sunrise; birth.

O.S.; o/s – old style calendar (see double-dating; Julian calendar).

Osrfd. (No) – Østfold.

o.t.p. – of this parrish.

oud–oom (Du) – eldest.

oudste (Du) – eldest.

oud–tante (Du) – grandaunt.

overgrootmoeder (Du) – great-grandmother.

overgrootvader (Du) – great-grandfather.

oxgang – a bovate (q.v.).

Oxon. (E) (L) – Oxford.

Oxonia, Oxonium, Oxenforda, Oxfordia, Oxonium (L) – Oxford.

P

p. – page; pater; per; populus; post; pro (qq.v.). *parents, *parentage.

Pa. – Pennsylvania.

p.a. – pro anno; per annum (qq.v.).

padre (It) (Sp) – father.

paese (It) – country.

page – one side of the leaf of a book, etc.; a boy servant or attendant; a youth in training for knighthood. Abbr.; p.; pp. – pages.

pais (Sp) – country.

päivä (Fi) – day.

palaeography – old or ancient writing; the science that treats of the writing of the ancients.

palatinate – a province or territory of the palatine or county palatine; a native or inhabitant of the Palatinate.

Palatinate – a state of the old German Empire, lying along the Rhine. The present Palatinate is a district of Bavaria.

palatine – of or pertaining to a palace; possessing royal privileges, as, a count or earl palatine; an officer of an imperial palace; a native or inhabitant of the Palatinate; a palatinate or county palatine.

Palatines of Pa. – early settlers, who through persecution were driven from their homes along the Rhine River, their home being called the Palatinate (q.v.).

palimpsest – a kind or portion of writing material, as parchment or paper, so prepared that the writing could be erased.

panoply – a full suit of armor; anything defending or protecting completely by covering or enveloping.

pam.; pamph. - pamphlet.

Papist - a Roman Catholic regarded as a partisan of the Pope.

Par. - Parish.

parens (L) -father; mother; parents.

parentis (L) - father; mother; parents.

parento (L)-to offer solemn sacrifice in honor of deceased parents or relatives; to revenge (a person's death by that of another).

parish - originally, in Great Britain and some British colonies, the ecclesiastical unit of area consisting of the circuit or district committed to the charge of one parson or vicar or other minister. Originally this district consisted of one or more vills or towns (in the south of England usually one, in the north several). Several parishes make up a Rural Deanery (q.v.).

parish register - a book kept for the recording of all the christenings, marriages, and burials in a parish. (see SYA p. 95; GGR p. 196; 4th Ed. HB p. 200). Abbr. - *P. R.

parocchia (It) - parish.

paroch - a clergymen in charge of a parish.

parochia (L) - parish.

parochie (Du) (G) (Ne) - parish.

parochial - of or pertaining to a parish.

paroisse (Fr) - parish.

parroquia (Sp) - parish.

parva (L) - little.

passenger list - a ship's list of passengers. Generally referring to the lists of passengers arriving in the U.S. from European countries. (see ABC p. 87).

passim (L) here and there, up and down, far and wide in a disorderly manner, confusedly.

pastor (L) - herdsman; shepherd.

pastorate (Sw) - recortal district containing more than one parish.

pat. - patent, patented.

patent - an instrument of deed making a conveyance or grant of public lands; the land of territory so conveyed.

patentee - one to whom a grant is made, or a privilege secured, by patent.

patent rolls - open or patent for all to read.

pater (L) - father; sire. Abbr. - p.

pater familias (L) - head of a household; father of a

family.

paternal – of or pertaining to a father.

patres (L.) – fathers. Abbr. – pp.

patria (L) – fatherland; native country.

Patricius (L) – Patrick.

patrius (L) – fatherly; paternal; hereditary; innate.

patronymic – in strict usage, a name formed by the addition of a prefix or suffix indicating sonship or other relationship to the name of one's father or paternal ancestor, as Johnson, son of John – Macdonald, son of Donald – Ivanovich, son of Ivan, etc.

patruelis (L) – cousin on the father's side.

patruus (L) – (paternal) uncle; severe reprover.

patruus major (L) – grandfather's brother (granduncle).

pauper (L) – poor man.

pays (Fr) – county or state.

P.C.C. – *Prerogative Court of Canterbury. (see prerogative court); privy council cases (q.v.).

Pc de C. (Fr) – Pas de Calais.

pchd. – *purchased.

P. C. Y. – *Prerogative Court of York, (see prerogative court).

peculiar parish – a parish which has been given the authority to administer its business without reference to the control of higher ecclesiastical authorities, such as deans, archdeacons and bishops. In some cases they had the right to probate a will.

peculium (L) – a small private property; private property of a son, daughter or slave, held with the father's or master's consent.

P. de D. (Fr) – Puy de Dome

pedigree – an ancestral line or line of descent; a genealogical table.

pedigree (Fr) – pedigree.

pedwerydd hen daid (W) – 4th great-grandfather.

P. E. I. – Prince Edward Island.

pellex (L) – concubine (of a married man).

Pembs. (W) – Pembroke.

Pennsylvania Dutch – descendants of 18th century settlers in Pa. from SW Germany; their dialect. (not Holland Dutch).

pension lists or records – the lists of pensioners who served in the wars of the U.S. from Revolutionary times on down. The Archivist of the United

States, National Archives Washington, D. C. has charge of pension applications (see SYA p. 119; ABC p. 85).

pentre (W) - village.

peo. - *people.

per (L) - by (means of); great; very; through; all over, etc. Abbr. - p.

per annum (L) - by the year; annually. Abbr. - p.a.

pere (Fr) - father.

peregrinus (L) - strange; stranger; foreigner.

perh. - perhaps.

personal property - estate or property that is not real, consisting in general, but not always, of things temporary or movable; chattels.

petite fille (Fr) - granddaughter.

petit fils (Fr) - grandson.

petition - a formally drawn-up request addressed to a person or a body of persons in authority or power, soliciting some favor, right, mercy, or other benefit. Abbr. - *petn.; *petitn.

petitioner - he who petitions Abbr. - *petr.

petitn. - *petition (q.v.).

petn. - *petition (q.v.).

petr. - *petitioner (q.v.).

Petronilla (L) - Parnel, Pernell.

Petrus (L) - Peter.

pfarramt (G) (Sz) - parish (the bounds of Catholic and Protestant parishes are different).

photostat copy - photographic cipies; copies of records, maps, etc., made with a photostat, one of the simpler methods of photographing any printed or handwritten material.

P. I. - The Republic of the Philippines.

pieni kaupunki (Fi) - small town.

pieni lansi (Fi) - infant.

pige (D) - girl.

pike (No) - girl.

Pilgrim Fathers - the English separatists who founded the colony of Plymouth, Mass., in 1620. (see Mayflower Compact)

pipe rolls - Eng. Hist., the great or annual, rolls containing the pipes or statements of the account of the king's revenue, expenses, etc., 1131 to 1833.

piscator (L) - fisherman.

pitäjä (Fi) - civil parish.

pl - public library

plaats (Ne) - place.

plantation - a place planted; an estate, usually large, and cultivated; in Maine, a minor civil division, having a very simple form of government; in Mass., land without trees of merchantable value.

plebes; plebs (L) – common people; populace.

plentyn (W) – infant, child.

plwyf (W) – parish.

poika (Fi) – boy, son.

pojanpoika (Fi) – grandson.

pojanpojanpoika, pojantyttarenpoika (Fi) – great-grandson.

pojanpojantytär, pojantyttärentytar (Fi) – great-granddaughter.

pojantytar (Fi) – granddaughter.

pojke (Sw) – boy.

Pomm. (G) – Pommern.

poor law – a law providing for or regulating support of the poor. Started in England 1601, in the U.S. at various times. (see GGR p. 227).

poor law union – see union.

popula (L) – people.

populus (L) – people. Abbr. – p.

post (L) – after, Abbr. – p.

Postal Guide – see U.S. Postal Guide.

posterity – descendants; offspring to the furthest generation.

postridie (L) – on the day after; the next day.

Potboiler – A book, painting etc., executed soley, and often hastily, as a means of subsistence.

potwaller – literally, pot-boiler; specif., Eng. Hist., one of a certain class of voters (see pot-walloper).

potwalloper – in certain boroughs of England before the Reform Act of 1832 a voter whose qualification for suffrage was the bolling (walloping) of his own pot, that is, the fact of being householder, as proved by his having a separate fireplace where food was cooked for himself and family.

power of attorney – an instument authorizing one to act as the attorney or agent of the person granting it either generally, or, more often, for some specified limited purpose Abbr. – p.p.a. (per power of attorney).

PP. – patres (q.v.).

pp. – pages (see page).

p.p.a. – per power of attorney (see power of attorney).

P. R. – Commonwealth of Puerto Rico.

P. R. – * parish register (q.v.).

praedium (L) – land; estate.

praenomen (L) – first name.

prec.; *precd. – preceding.

predecessore (It) – ancestor.

predicator – preacher; esp., a preaching friar.

pre-emption – act or right of purchasing before others; a piece of land occupied under a pre-emption right. (q.v.).

Pre-Emption Application – an application by a person who had already settled on unappropriated land.

pre-emption right – right given by the Federal public land laws (repealed 1891) to citizens of buy-in a quarter section of land or less. (see pre-emption).

prerogative court – formerly, the court of either of the archbishops (of Canterbury or York in Eng., or Armagh in Ireland), which had juris-diciton in all cases of will or administrations, transferred to Court of Probate 1857; the probate court of New Jersey.

preussisch (G) – Prussian.

pridem (L) – long since.

pridie (L) – on the day before.

prima (Sp) – female cousin.

primo (Sp) – male cousin.

primogénito (It) Sp) – eldest, firstborn.

primos hermanos (Sp) – first cousins.

primos segundos (Sp) – second cousins.

priod, prioddodd (W) – married.

priores (L) – ancestors.

Private Land Claim – a claim to land granted to individuals from foreign countries prior to the cession of that land to the U.S. These were in Ala., Ark., Calif., Fla., Ill., Ind., Iowa, La., Mich., Miss., Mo., Colo and N. Mex.

privigna (L) – stepdaughter.

privignus (L) – stepson.

privy council – a secret council; a private, or personal council.

pro (L) – for. Abbr. – p.

pro. – *probate; *proved.

Pro. *Province.

P. R. O. – *Public Record Office.

pro anno (L) – for the year. Abbr. – p.a.

proavia (L) – great-grand-mother.

proavus (L) – great grand-father; ancestor.

prob. – probably.

probate – proof; official proof; esp., the proof before a tribunal that an instrument offered is the last will and testament of a person deceased. (see probate court).

probate court - a court for the probate of wills, administration of estates and related matters (see probate).

professional genealogist - one engaged in genealogical research as a vocation; one receiving remuneration for genealogical work. (see amateur genealogist).

progenies (L) - race; family; progeny.

progenitor - an ancestor; a forefather.

progenitores (Sp) - progenitors, ancestors.

proles (L)-offspring; progeny; descendants.

pronepos (L) - great grandson.

proneptis (L) - great-granddaughter.

pronipota (f) (It) - great-granddaughter.

pronipote(m) (It) - great-grandson.

pronurus (L) - wife of a grandson.

proof - an establishment of a fact by evidence.

proofread - to read and mark corrections in; to read in order to detect and mark errors.

prop. - property.

propositus - one whose relations are sought to be ascertained by a genealogical table; intestate.

propr. - proprietor(s).

prosapia (L)-family; pedigree; race.

proved will - a will established as genuine by probate court.

Province - an ecclesiastical jurisdiction comprising a number of dioceses or bishoprics as they are sometimes called, coming under the jurisdiction of an archbishop. There are three in England - Canterbury, York and Wales.

province - an administrative unit of a country; a region of country; a district.

provincia (It) (L) - county, province.

provincie (Du) (Ne) - province, district.

Provinz (G) - province.

provis. - *provision.

provost - a person appointed to superintend, or preside over, something; a person appointed as an official head.

proximo (L) - next month.

Prudentia (L) - Prudence.

ptf. - *plaintiff.

pub. - public; published; publisher.

public domain - public lands.

pueblo (Sp) - small town.

puella (L) – girl; sweetheart.

puer (L) – child; boy; young man.

pupillus (L) – orphan boy.

Puritan – one of a class of Protestants who arose in the 16th century within the church of England. Because of religious persecution many left their homes forming a large segment of the early population of New England. (see Mayflower Compact; Pilgrim Fathers).

pursuivant – a heraldic officer ranking below a herald; an official attendant of the heralds.

putative – commonly regarded as such; supposed as a putative father.

putilla (L) – little girl.

putillus (L) – little boy.

pymt. – payment.

Pyr.Orient. (Fr) – Pyrenees Orientales.

Q

q.e. – quod est (q.v.).

qq. v. – quae vide (q.v.).

quadrimus (L) – of four years, four years old.

quae spondet infantis loco (L) – godmother.

quae vide (L) – which see (plural). Abbr. – qq.v.

Quaker – see Friends.

Que. – Quebec.

que (L) – and (used only as an enclitic particle).

quod (L) – that, in that, because; wherefore; although.

quod est (L) – which is. Abbr. – q.e.

quod vide (L) – which see (singular). Abbr. – q.v.

q.v. – quod vide (q.v.).

qy. – query.

R

R.; r. – rector; regins; rex. (qq.v.).

Radnors. (W) – Radnor.

Radulfus (L) – Ralph.

Raga, Ragae, Rhage, Rage (L) – Leicester.

ragazza (It) – girl.

ragazzo (It) – boy.

Rang. (Ic) – Rangarvallasysla.

rat. – *rated.

R.C. – Roman Catholic.

rcdr. – recorder.

re. – *regarding.

reading machine – the machine used for reading microfilms (q. v.). It makes an enlarged image on ground glass. (ABC p. 33).

real estate or property – land and whatever by nature or artificial annexation is part of it or is the means of its enjoyment, as minerals, trees buildings, fences, etc.

rec. - record; recorder.

rector - a clergyman; the ruler or governor of a country; the chief. Abbr. - R.; r.

Redemptioner - one who, wishing to emigrate from Europe to America secured passage on credit, binding himself to be sold into service by the master or owner of the ship for a stipulated time.

reg.- register

Reg. Gen. - Registrar General (q.v.).

regina (L) - queen, Abbr.- R.; r.

register - a book in which entries of acts, occurrences, names, or the like are recorded; a book or system of public records.

Registrar General - the head of any general register office; spec., Eng., the chief official of the General Register Office, Somerset House, London, W.C.2, England.

regius (L) - kingly, royal, regal.

rel. - relative; religion; released.

relationship - connection or alliance by blood or marriage; kinship.

relative-in-law - one who is related by marriage. Abbr. - *rel-i-l.

relic - widow, usually followed by "of"; remains.

relict (L) - survivor; widow.

relicta (L) - widow.

relictus (L) - widower.

rel-i-l. - *relative-in-law (q.v.).

rep. - report; representative.

repository - a place, room, etc., where things are deposited or stored; such as: a museum, an archive a burial vault, etc.

repud. - *repudiate.

requiescat in pace (L) - may he or she rest in peace. Abbr. - R.I.P.

res. -research; residence; resides.

Rev. - *Revolutionary War. (q.v.); Reverend.

rev. - revised.

Revolutionary War - the war of the American revolution, 1775-83. *Rev.; Rev. War; R. W.

Rev. War. - Revolutionary War (q.v.).

rex (L) -king; tyrant; master; leader; tutor. Abbr. -R.: r.

rgstr. - registrar.

Rhinel. (G) - Rheinland or Rheinprovinz.

R.I. - Rhode Island.

Ricardus (L) – Richard.

riding – an administrative district, orig., York, Eng., but also found in other British Colonies and at one time in Pennsylvania and Long Island; divison of the county in Yorkshire comprising a number of wapentakes; from the Saxon triding, i.e., third part. There are the East, North and West Ridings in Yorkshire.

Ringkby (D) – Ringkøbing.

R.I.P. – requiescat in pace (q.v.).

rlnq.– *relinquished.

Robertus (L) – Robert.

Roesia, Rosa, Rosia (L) – Rose.

Rogald. (No) – Rogaland.

Rogerus (L) – Roger.

Roman Numerals – numerals in the Roman system of notation with values as follows:

I or i – one (see J.).
II or ii – two
III or iii – three
IV or iv – four
V or v – five
VI or vi – six
VII or vii – seven
VIII or viii – eight
IX or ix – nine
X or x – ten
L – fifty
C – one hundred
D – five hundred
M – one thousand

The Roman numeral I, when it stands alone, is number one; when it is placed before another numeral it subtracts one; when it is placed after another numeral it adds one. It is the same with other numerals, if they are placed in front of a numeral of greater value their value is subtracted, if after, their value is added.

Suppose you should write 1953 in Roman numerals. Always the largest number is written first (unless you want to subtract), and the smaller numbers in sequence. In this case the largest number is 1000 which is M. the next largest is 900 which is CM. The third largest number is 50, which is L. The last number is 3 which is III. Hence, 1953 is written MCMLIII.

Suppose you see the letters MDCLXXXV you would say; M – 1000, D – 500, C – 100 (ΓC–600), L – 50, XXX – 30, (LXXX – 80), and V – 5. Thus, MDCLXXXV – 1685.

Suppose the letters you write down are MDCCC XXXIX. M - 1000, D - 500, CCC - 300, XXX - 30, IX - 9, total 1839.

At one time the letter "K" was used for 250 and "G" for 400.

Romish Priest - a priest of Rome.

Roscom. (Ire) - Rosecommon.

Ross & Crom. (Sc) - Ross & Cromarty.

Rotelandia (L) - Rutland.

rovastikunta (Fi) - rural deanery.

Roxb. (Sc) - Roxburgh.

Rural Deanery - see deanery.

ruricola (L) - husbandman.

rus (L) - country; countryseat; farm.

rustica (L) - country girl.

rusticus (L) - rural.

Rutlanda(ia) (L) - Rutlandshire.

Rutlds. (E) - Rutland.

RW - *Revolutionary War. (q.v.).

S

s. - sepultus; son; *spinster (qq.v.); *sons; successor.

s.a. (L) - secundum artem; sine anno (q.v.).

sa. (Her) - sable; black.

sadt (G) - town, city.

Salopesbiria, Salopia (L) -

Shrewsbury, In Shropshire.

Salopescira (L) - Shropshire.

Salzbg. (Aus) - Salzburg.

s and coh - *son and coheir

s and h - *son and heir.

S.A.R. - Sons of the American Revolution.

Sask. - Saskatchewan.

Saxe. (G) - Sachsen or Saxe.

S.C. - South Carolina.

Scand. - Scandinavian.

scatt. - *scattering or *scattered.

Sch./Lippe (G) - Schaumburg/Lippe.

Schles./Holst. (G) - Schleswig/Holstein.

Schwarzw. (G) - Schwarzwald.

schwester (G) sister.

Scot. - Scotland.

Scotus (L) - Scotchman.

script - handwriting; the characters used in handwriting; a writing.

Scutage - payment of money in place of military service.

S.C.V. - Sons of Confederate Veterans.

S. Dak. - South Dakota.

sec. - second; secretary; section; sector.

sec. - security.

seisen - possession of either land or chattel. Also seizen.

seized of - legally possessed of.

Selk. (Sc) – Selkirk.

Sen. – senior (q.v.).

senecta; senectus (L) – old age.

senex (L) – old man; old woman; aged.

senior – older or elder. Abbr. – Sen.; Sr. (see junior for instability of use).

senium (L) – old age.

Sennachie (Sc) – tribal genealogist of Scottish Clans.

señorita (Sp) – young unmarried lady.

senza marito, smaritato (It) unmarried.

sep. – sepultus (q.v.).

separatist – One who withdraws from a church; a seceder from an established church; a dissenter; nonconformist.

seppolto (It) – buried.

sept – a branch of a Scottish highland clan.

sepulcrum (L) – grave.

sepulta (L) – buried.

sepultado (Sp) – buried.

sepultus (L) – buried. Abbr. – s.; sep.

seqq. – sequentia (q.v.).

sequentia (L) – the following, Abbr. – seqq.

ser. – *servant; *service.

serf – a person the property of another.

serg. – sergeant.

serkku (Fi) – cousin.

serv.; servt. – servant.

serva (L) – maid servant.

servula (L) – servant girl.

servulus (L) – servant lad.

servus (L) – servant; slave.

setä (Fi) – uncle.

S./et L. (Fr) – Saone-et-Loire.

S./et M. (Fr) – Seine-et-Marne.

S./et' O. (Fr) – Seine'et' Oise.

settl. – *settled; *settler.

seurakunta (Fi) – church parish.

sev. – *several.

Sevenbg. (D) – Svendborg.

S/Fjord (No) – Sogn og Fjordane.

sh. – *share; *ship.

shield – the escutcheon or field on which are placed the bearings in coats of arms (q.v.).

shire – a county; one of the counties of Great Britain.

Shrops. (E) – Shropshire.

Sibella (L) – Sybil.

sic (L) – thus; to show that a quoted passage, often containing some error, is precisely reproduced.

Sidneus (L) – Sidney.

signator (L) – signer; witness (to a will).

signatura (L) – signature.

Siluanus (L) – Silas.

sin. – sine (q.v.).

sine (L) – without. Abbr. –

Sn.; sin.

sine anno (L) - without year. Abbr. - s.a.

sine loco (L) - without place. Abbr. - s.l.

sine loco, anno, velnomine (L) - without place, year or name. Abbr. - s.l.a.n.

sine prole (L) - without issue; without children. Abbr. - s.p.

sine prole supersite (L) - without surviving issue (children). Abbr. - s.p.s.

sir (W) - county.

Sir - the distinctive title of a knight or baronet; a title of respect for some notable personage of ancient times.

sîr, swydd (W) - shire, county.

*sis.; sist. - sister (q.v.).

sisar (Fi) - sister.

sisarenpoika (Fi) - sister's son (nephew).

sisarukset (Fi) - brothers and sisters.

sis.il.; sis-i-l - *sister-in-law (q.v.).

sister - the daughter of the same parents; a female friend; a female member of a religious community (nun); a nurse in charge of a hospital room. Abbr. - *sis; sist.

sister-in-law - one's husband's or wife's sister; one's brother's wife.

Abbr. - *sis.il.; *sis-i-l; *sister-i-l.

Skag. (Ic) - Skagafjardarsysla.

Skanbg. (D) - Skanderborg.

Skarabg. (Sw) - Skaraborg.

skeppslag (Sw) - coastal government area.

s.l. - sine loco (q.v.).

slaegteregister (D) - pedigree.

s.l.a.n. - sine loco, anno, vel nomine (q.v.).

s.l.p. (L) - sine legitima prole; without legitimate issue.

S.Manld. (Sw) - Södermanland.

S.Marit. (Fr) - Seine-Maritime.

S.Mul. (Ic) - Sudur-Mulasysla.

Sn. - sine (q.v.).

Snaef. (Ic) - Snaefellsnessysla.

s/o - *son of.

sobrina; sobrinus (L) - first cousin; cousin - german; (Sp) niece.

sobrino (Sp) - nephew.

soc. - society

socer; socerus (L) - father-in-law.

soceri (L) - parents-in-law

Society of Friends - see Friends.

söcken (Sw) - civil or political parish.

socrus (L) - mother-in-law.

soeur (Fr) - sister.

sogn (No) - parish.

sogne (D) - parish.

sohn (G) - son.

So. Holl. (Ne)-Zuid Holland (South Holland).

Sokn (Ic) - parish.

sol. - *soldier.

soltero (Sp) - unmarried.

Som. (E) - Somerset.

Somersata, Somerseta, Somersetania, Somersetensis, Somertunensis Comitatus, Sumersetanea, Sumertunensis, Summurtunensis Paga (L) - Somersetshire.

Somerset House - where the registers of births, marriages, and deaths of England and Wales (1837) to present) are kept. Somerset House, London, W.C.2, England.

son - male child or person in relation to his parents; one adopted as a son; a familiar term of address. (see SYA p. 139).

son (Sw) - son.

Søn (D) - son.

sondotter(Sw)-son's daughter (granddaughter).

son.il.; son-i-l(q.v.) - *son-in-law.

son-in-law - the husband of one's daughter; a stepson.

sønn (No) - son.

sønnedatter (D) - son's daughter(granddaughter).

sønne-datter (No) - son's daughter (granddaughter).

sønnesøn (D) - son's son (grandson).

sønne-sønn (No) - son's son (grandson).

sønnesønsdatter (D)-son's son's daughter (great-grand-daughter).

sønnesønssøn (D) - son's son's son (great-grandson).

sonson (Sw) - son's son (grandson).

sonsons dotter (Sw) - son's son's daughter (great-granddaughter).

sonsons son (Sw) - son's son's son (great-grandson).

sorella (It) - sister.

soror (L) - sister; female companion or friend. Abbr. - Sr.

sororis (L) - sister.

sororis filia - see filia sororis.

søster (No) (D) - sister.

søsterdatter (D) - sister's daughter (niece).

søstersøn (D) - sister's son (nephew).

sou. - *south, southern.

source references - references to books, mss., registers, publications, etc., wherein is found the information on which the author has based his premise or writings. (see GGR p. 221).

Southeria (L) - Surrey.

Southsexena (L) - The County of Sussex.

s.p., (L) - sine prole; without issue. (q.v.).

späadbarn (Sw) - infant.

späadebarn (D) - infant.

spebarn (No) - infant.

spell. - *spelling; *spelled.

spinster - a woman still unmarried; one who spins. Abbr. - *S. *spr.

sponsor (L) - bondsman; surety. Abbr. -*spr.; *S.

sponsus (L) - betrothed; bridegroom; suitor.

sposa (It) - wife.

sposo (It) - husband.

spr. - *spinster; *sponsor (qq.v.).

s.p.s. - sine prole supersite (q.v.).

spurius (L) - illegitimate child or birth.

Sr. - senior; soror (qq.v.).

Sr. (before a Name) - Sir.

srnms. - *surnames.

S.S. - supra scriptum (q.v.).

SS. - Santi (It) - Saints.

Sta. - Santa (It)-Saint, fem

staat (G) - state.

stad (D) (Du) (Ne) (No) (Sw) - city.

stadt (G) (Sz) - city, town.

stadtgemeinde (G) - urban municipality.

Staffordia, Staffordsc' (L)- Staffordshire.

Staffs (E) - Stafford.

stamfader (D) (Sw) - an-cestor.

stamfar (No) - progenitor, ancestor.

stamtavia (Sw) - pedigree.

stamtavle (No) -genealogical table.

stamtre (No) - pedigree, genealogical tree.

standesamt (G) - civil registrar's office.

starb (G) - died.

starb kinderlos (G) - died without issue.

State of Franklin - see Franklin, State of.

Status Plat - a copy of the plat or survey upon which has been diagrammed and noted such information as is necessary to determine the Federal ownership of public lands and resources.

Steafordensis (L) - Of Stafford.

Steierm.(Aus) -Steiermark

stemma, stemma gentile (L) - pedigree.

Steofordensis (L) - Of Stafford.

step - a prefix indicating connection between members of a family by the remarriage of a parent, and not by blood. (see SYA p. 140).

stepchild - a child of one's husband or wife by a former marriage. (see step)

stepfather - the husband by

remarriage of one's mother.

Stephanus (L) – Stephen.

S. Thing. (Ic) – Sudur Thingeyjarsysla.

stift or biskopsstift (Sw) – bishopric or diocese containing a number of rural deaneries.

still born – dead when born.

stirps – stock; race, family, or branch of family. In law – the person from whom a family or branch of a family is descended. Pl. stirpes.

Stockhm. (Sw) – Stockholm.

Strand. (Ic) – Strandasysla.

S. Tronlg. (No) – Sør Trøndelag.

subnuba (L) – second wife; intruder; rival.

Sudovolca, Suffolcia, Suffolicia (L) – Suffolk.

Sudria (L) – Surrey.

Sudsexa (L) – Sussex.

Suff. (E) – Suffolk.

Suffolca (L) – Suffolk.

sukupuu (Fi) – pedigree.

sukutaulu (Fi) – pedigree.

Sumersetanea, Sumertunensis, Summurtunensis Paga (L) – Somersetshire.

sup. – superior

supra scriptum (L) – written above. Abbr. – S.S.

supt. – superintendent.

surg. – surgeon.

surname – the name which a person has in common with the other members of his family, as distinguished from his Christian or given name; a family name.

surname file or catalogue – the card index of a genealogical library listing surnames (q.v.).

Surr. (E) – Surrey, Surrogate.

Surra, Surria, Surreia (L) – Surrey.

susceptor (L) – undertaker; receiver; godfather.

Suss. (E) – Sussex.

Sussexia (L) – Sussex.

Suth. (Sc) – Sutherland.

Suthamtunensis Provincia (L) – Hampshire.

Suthregia, Suthreia (L) – Surrey.

Suthriona (L) – Surrey.

Suthsaxonia (L) – Sussex.

Suthsexia (L) – Sussex.

suus (L) – his own, her own its own, their own.

S.U.V. – Sons of Union Veterans.

S.V. – Sons of Veterans.

sw. – *swear; *swore.

Sw. – Sweden, Swedish.

swydd (W) – county.

symbols used by genealogists in Continental Europe appear on many pedigrees and family records. Some, if not all those listed below, might well be used by American genealogists. The following have been checked from several sources and are the most common - you may find many others.

born - * or X
born illegitimate - (*)
christened - ⌐ or =
betrothed - o
married - oo or ∞
divorced - o/o
common law marriage o-o
died - ⊤ or ⊹ or /
died of battle wounds - ⊹ ✄
died in battle - ✄ or XX
burial ▭ or ◻ or ◻
no further issue - ⫫ or (⊹)
cremation - ◡
syntynty (Fi) - born.
syskon (Sw) - brothers and sisters.
sysla (Ic) - county.
syster (Sw) - sister.
systerdotter (Sw) - sister's daughter (niece).
systerson (Sw) - sister's son (nephew).

T

t. -tempore; tomus (qq.v.).
tabularium (L) - archives; register-office.
tad (W) - father.
tag (G) - day.
taid (W) - grandfather.
tak. - *taken.

tante (D) (Du) (Fr) (G) (No) - aunt.
tartan - woolen cloth, checkered or cross barred with narrow bands of various colors, much worn in the Scottish Highlands, where each clan had its distinctive tartan.
tatarabuela (Sp)-2nd great-grandmother.
tatarabuelo (Sp)-2nd great-grandfather.
täti (Fi) - aunt.
tectum (L) - house; abode; dwelling.
Telemk. (No) - Telemark.
temp. - tempore (q.v.).
tempore (L) - in the time of. Abbr. - t.; temp.
tempus (L) - time; season; occasion.
ten, tenne (Her) - a stain.
Tenn. - Tennessee.
Terr. - Territory.
Terr. Belf. (Fr) - Terri-toire de Belfort.
test. - testament (q.v.).
testament (Du) (E) (Fr) (G) a formal declaration, usually in writing, of a person's wishes as to the disposition of his property after his death; formerly, a disposition to take effect upon death and relating to personal property (as distinguished from real property), but now will and testa-

ment are synonymous. (see will; nuncupative).

testamenta (D) - will, testament.

testamente (No) (Sw) -will, testament.

testamento (It) (Sp) - will, testament.

testamentti (Fi) - will, testament.

testamentum (L) - will; testament.

testate - having made and left a valid will.

testator - one who leaves a valid will.

testatrix - a female testator.

T. et' G. (Fr) - Tarn et' Garonne.

Tex. Texas.

T.H. - Territory of Hawaii

tho. - *though.

Thomasina (L) -Thomasine Tamsin.

thot. - *thought.

thro. - *through.

tía (Sp) - aunt.

tía abuela (Sp) - grandaunt.

tibicen (L) - fluteplayer; piper.

til. - *until.

tila (Fi) - small farm.

Timotheus (L) - Timothy.

tingslag (Sw) -sub-division of a judicial district.

tío (Sp) - uncle.

tío abuelo (Sp) -granduncle.

tipoldefader (D)-2nd great-grandfather.

Tipp. (Ire) - Tipperary.

tippoldefar (No)-2nd great-grandfather.

tippoldemor (No) - 2nd great grandmother.

tipp-tippoldefar (No) - 3rd great-grandfather.

tipp-tippoldemor (No) -3rd great-grandmother.

tipp-tipp-tippoldefar (No)- 4th great-grandfather.

tiptipoldefader (D) - 3rd great-grandfather.

tiptiptipoldefader (D) - 4th great-grandfather.

tithing - a small administrative division locally preserved in many parts of England apparently originally consisting of ten men with their families, or the tenth part of a hundred (q.v.).

tithingman - the chief man of a tithing (q.v.).

tochter (G) - daughter.

tomus (L) - volume; tome; one volume of a larger work. Abbr. - t.

tonsor (L) - barber; haircutter.

Tory - a person living in the American colonies during the Revolution who remained loyal to Great Britain; a major political party in Great Britain.

town - may refer to an abode or house, a small group of houses, a village, or on up to a large city, according to its usage at various times and places.

township - the inhabitants of, or a vill, manor or medieval town; a social or tribal unit among the Anglo-Saxons; an administrative district similar to a parish; in the U.S., (mostly) a tract of land which is a geographical rather than a political division. Abbr.- tp.; twp.

tp. - township (q.v.).

t.p. - title page.

t.p.m. - title page mutilated

t.p.w. - title page wanting.

Tract Book - a narrative journal like record which is an index to and digest of all essential actions and transactions which effect public lands. District Land Office Tract Books list individual entries by range and township.

tradition - the handing down of statements, beliefs, legends, customs, genealogies, etc., from generation to generation, esp. by word of mouth.

transcr. - *transcribed.

transcribe - to make a copy of in writing.

transcript - a reproduction in writing or print.

tre (W) - town.

treas. - treasurer

tref (W) - town.

Trenovantum (L) - London.

trial docket - a book or record containing the list of causes to be tried in court.

tritavus (L) - great grandfather's great grandfather.

trolovede (D) - engaged, betrothed.

tr.; trans. - translated, translation.

trustee - orig., a person regarded with trust or to whom something is entrusted; now, one trusted to keep or administer something.

trydydd hendaid (W) - 3rd great-grandfather.

tumulo (L) - to bury; to inter; to entomb.

tumulus (L) - mound; grave; monument; urn.

Tuomiokunta (Fi) - judicial district or judicial circuit.

Turstanus (L) - Thurstan.

Tvl.-Transvaal (So.Africa).

twn. - town.

twp. - township (q.v.).

tytär (Fi) - daughter.

tyttärenpoika (Fi) - daughter's son (grandson).

tyttärenpojanpoika (Fi) - daughter's son's son, (great-grandson).

tyttärenpojantytär (Fi) – daughter's son's daughter (great-granddaughter).

tyttärentytär (Fi) – daughter's daughter (granddaughter).

tyttärentyttärenpoika (Fi) – daughter's daughter s son (great-grandson).

tyttö (Fi) – girl.

U

u. – used interchangeably with "v" in Old English.

uägte (D) – illegitimate.

U.C. – Upper Canada.

uekte (No) – illegitimate.

ugift (D) (No) – unmarried.

U.K. – United Kingdom.

ult. – ultimo (q.v.).

ulter (L) – placed at a greater distance; farther; worse.

ultimo (L) – in the mouth preceding the present. Abbr. – ult.; ulto.

ultimus – last, end, furthest

ulto. – ultimo (q.v.).

Umfridus (L) – Humfrey.

uncle – a brother of one's mother or father; husband of one's aunt; a familiar title or title of endearment applied to an older man.

uncle–i–l. – *uncle–in–law (q.v.).

uncle–in–law – the uncle of

one's husband or wife; the husband of one's aunt. Abbr. – *uncle–i–l.

unehelich (G) – illegitimate

ungkarl (D) – bachelor.

unigena (L) – only–begotten; only; of one family.

unigenitus (L) – the only son.

union – a registration district in England and Wales, comprising two or more parishes, also called poor–law union.

unit. – *united; *uniting.

unk. – *unknown.

unm. – *unmarried.

unorg. – unorganized

unter – (G) – lower.

Unterfr. (G) –Unterfranken

unverheiratet (G) – unmarried.

uomo (It) – man.

urbs (L) – a walled town; city; citizens.

urenkel (G) – great–grandson.

urenkelin (G) – great–granddaughter.

urgrossmutter (G) – great–grandmother.

urgrossvater (G) – great–grandfather.

2ter urgrossvater (G) –2nd great–grandfather.

3ter urgrossvater (G) –3rd great–grandfather.

4ter urgrosvater (G) – 4th great–grandfather.

Urovicum (L) – York.

U. S. Postal Guide - the official guide published by the U.S. Post Office, giving the complete list of post offices in the United States and territories. Published yearly. It is called "Directory of Post Offices."

ut (L) - in what manner, how; in the manner that, as; how ever, etc.

ux.; uxor - wife (q.v.).

uxor (L) - wife; spouse; consort. Abbr. - ux.

uxoris (L) - wife.

V

v - used interchangeably with "u" in Old English.

V., v. - volume.

Va. - Virginia.

v.a. - vixit annos (q.v.).

vader (Du) - father.

Vadum Rubrum (L) - Hertford.

V./Agder.(No) - Vest/Agder

vaimo (Fi) - wife.

vanha (Fi) - aged, old.

vanhin (Fi) - eldest.

var. - variation; various.

Varmld. (Sw) - Värmland.

Varvicum (L) - Warwick.

vater (G) - father.

V./Bard. (Ic) - Vestur/ Bardastrandarsysla.

V./bottn. (Sw)-Västerbotten

vecchio (It) - aged.

vedova (It) - widow.

vedovo (It) - widower.

vel (L) - or; even, even as; at least, etc.

veli (Fi) - brother.

veljenpoka (Fi) - brother's son (nephew).

veljentytär (Fi) - brother's daughter (niece).

Venantodunia (L) - Huntingdonshire.

verbatim - word for word; in the same words; verbally.

verch (W) -daughter (properly merch).

verheiratet (G) - married.

Verouicum (L) - Warwick.

Verovicum (L) - Warwick.

vert, Vert (Her) - green.

Vervicum (L) - Warwick.

Vestfd. (No) - Vestfold.

Vestm. (Ic) - Vestmannaeyjasysla.

vetter (G) - cousin.

vetula (L) - little old woman.

vetulus (L) - little old man.

vetus (L) - aged; old.

veuf (Fr) - widower.

veuve (Fr) - widow.

V./Hun. (Ic) - Vestur/ Hunavatnssysla.

viator (L) - traveller; a runner or messenger attached to a magistrates service.

vicar - a person acting as priest of a parish in place of a rector; a clergyman.

vicarage - the residence of

a vicar; the office or duties of a vicar.

vicaria (L) – vicarage (q.v.)

viculus (L) – little village; hamlet.

vicus (L) – a ward or district of a city; a village; a hamlet.

vide (L) – see.

videlicet (L) – it is easy to see; that is to say; to whit; namely. Abbr. – viz.

video (L) – see.

vidius (L) – living; true to life; vigorous.

vidnere (D) – witnesses.

vidua (L) – widow.

viduata (L) – widowed.

viduus (L) – widower; widow; deprived of or separated from something.

viejo (Sp) – aged.

Vigornia (L) – Worcester.

vil(l)icus (L) – steward; overseer of an estate; balliff; of or belonging to an estate.

village – a small aggregation of houses in the country, being in general less in number than a town or city and more than a hamlet.

village (Fr) – village.

ville (Fr) – city or town.

villein – a serf (q.v.)

villie (D) – will.

villingen (G) – Villingen.

Vilugiana Provincia (L) – Wiltshire.

vintner – one who deals in wine.

vir; viri (L) – man; boy; male; husband; soldier.

virgate – O.E. term meaning 1/4 acre, or sometimes 1/4 carcute (30 acres). Probably other meanings.

virgo (L) – maid; virgin; girl.

viri – see vir.

Vis. – viscount (q.v.) or viscountess.

Visc. – viscount (q.v.). or viscountess.

viscount – an officer who formerly acted in place of the count, or earl; a sheriff. Abbr. – Vis.; Visc; Visct.

Visct. – viscount (q.v.). or viscountess.

V.Isf. (Ic) – Vestur-Isafjardarsysla.

visitation – an official personal inquiry made by an officer-at-arms at different times to examine the rights of the people within his heraldic province to bear arms; the record of such inquiry. (see Herald's College, heraldry, etc.).

visitation pedigree – the pedigrees copied by the herald in his book of "visitations" (q.v.).

vit. – vital.

vital records or statistics - records or statistics relating to birth, deaths, marriages health and disease. Abbr. - *V.R.

viuda (Sp) - widow

viudo (Sp) - widower.

vivus (L) - alive; living; natural.

vixit annos (L) - he or she lived—years. Abbr. -v.a.

viz. - videlicet. (q.v.)

VL. - Vulgar Latin.

V⁄Manld. (Sw) - Västmanland.

V⁄Norld. (Sw) - Västernorrland.

vol. - volume.

voorvader (Du) - ancestor, forefather.

Vorarlbg. (Aus) - Vorarlberg.

vorder (G) - anterior.

vorfahre (G) - ancestor, forefather.

v.p. - in father's lifetime.

V.R. - *vital records.

vrouw (Du) - wife.

VS.- *vital statistics.

V. Skaft. (Ic) - Vestur⁄ Skaftafellssysla.

Vt. - Vermont.

vuosi (Fi) - year

vixor (L) - wife - see uxor also "V".

W

w. - wife; *widow.

1/w, 2/w - first wife, second wife, etc.

wald (G) - forest.

Waldsh. (G) - Waldshut.

wapentake - a division corresponding to a hundred and ward (qq.v.) of some English counties; the court of such division; the bailiff serving this court.

ward - in the counties of Cumberland and Northcumberland, and in some Scottish counties, a division answering to the hundred and wapentake (qq.v.) of other counties. Wards are often merely or chiefly the divisions of a city for election purposes.

Warewichscira (L) - Warwickshire.

Warning Out Law - a colonial law which empowered a town to warn out individuals or families that were newcomers (within 3 years) and had become impoverished and likely to become town charges, to return to the town from whence they came. No stigma was attached to this procedure; sometimes a widow with children was warned out after her husbands death, if she did not have means of supporting her family.

Warrant – to guarantee to a purchaser or other grantee, the title to, or quality, or quantity of, the thing sold or granted, as a warranty deed.

Warwicus (L) – Warwick.

Warws. (E) – Warwick.

Wash. – Washington.

Waterfd. (Ire) – Waterford.

WB. – *Will Book.

wd. – *widow.

weduwe (Du) – widow.

weduwnaar (Du) – widower.

wendisch, windisch (G) – slavic.

Wenta (L) – Monmouth.

west. – *western

Westmaria (L) – Westmorland.

Westmd. (E) – Westmorland.

Westmoria, Westmorlandia (L) – Westmorland.

Westph. (G) – Westfalen.

Wexfd. (Ire) – Wexford.

W. Fland. (Bel) – West Vlaanderen.

wf/o.– *wife of.

wh. – *who; *which.

Whig – a political party which was in opposition to the Tories in Great Britain until 1832; also in Colonial America, the Whig Party was opposed to British rule and to the Tories.

Wiccia (L) – Worecestershire.

Wickl. (Ire) – Wicklow.

wid. – *widow.

Wigornia (L) – Worcester.

Wilhelmus (L) – William.

will – the legal declaration of a person's mind as to the manner in which he would have his property or estate disposed of after his death; the term testament (q.v.), originally a Roman and Civil law term, is often now used as synonymous with will. A will or testament may be nuncupative (q.v.) or written. (see SR pp. 12, 13, 16, 17; SYA pp. 11, 84-94; 1953 HB pp. 2, 149, 218; ABC p. 38; GGR pp. 84-89).

Wiltescira, Wiltonia (L) – Wiltshire.

Wilts. (E) – Wiltshire.

windisch (G) – see wendisch.

Wis. – Wisconsin.

wit. – *witness, *witnessed.

witness – one who gives testimony as in a court of law; one who signs a document in attestation of the genuineness of its execution; a sponsor at baptism. Abbr. – *wtn.

witwe (G) – widow.

witwer (G) – widower.

wk. – week; work.

wks. – weeks; works.

W. Lothian (Sc) – West Lothian.

W. Meath (Ire) – West Meath

wnt. – *wants.

W/o.– *wife of.

Worcs. (E) – Worcester.

WPA Historical Records Survey – a program undertaken by the U.S. Government in 1936–43 in which inventories were compiled of historical material, particular unpublished government documents and records which are basic in the administration of local government, and which provide much data for students of political, economic and social history. (see ABC p. 55; 4th Ed HB p. VIII).

W. P. – *will probated.

W. Pruss. (G) – West-preussen (incl. Danzig).

Writer to the Signet (Sc) – Scottish Legal Profession, equivalent to English solicitor (lawyer) Abbr. W.S.

W. S. – Writer to the Signet (q.v.).

wtn. – *witness (q.v.).

Wuertt. (G) – Wuerttemberg.

W. Va. – West Virginia.

ww. – *widow.

Ww/O – *widow of.

wwr. – *widower.

Wyo. – Wyoming.

wyr (W) – grandson, grand-child.

wyres (W) – granddaughter.

X

X – is used to designate an ancestor (q.v.) on some family group sheets

X, – Christ; christian (properly the Greek letter chi. which in form is like X); on pedigrees X is sometimes a symbol for born.

xch.– *exchange.

Xn. – Christian.

Xnty. – Christianity.

Xped. – *christened.

Xper.; Xr. – Christopher.

Xpoferus (L) – Christopher.

Xt. – Christ (see X,).

Xtian. – Christian.

Xty. – Christianity.

Y

y. – year or years.

ye – the (Old English): plural of thou; used for the objective of "you."

yeo – *yeoman; yeomanry (qq.v.).

Yeogerieceastrie (L) – Worcester.

yeoman – a servant, attendant, or subordinate official in royal or other great household; a subordinate of a sheriff; an independant farmer.

Abbr. – *yeo.

yeomanry – the position or rank of a yeoman; the collective body of small landed proprietors of the middle class. Abbr. – yeo.

yngst (No) (Sw) – youngest.

yngste (D) – youngest.

Yorks. (E) – Yorkshire.

yr. – year; younger; your.

yrs. – years; yours.

Yukon – Yukon Territory.

Z

zia (It) – aunt.

zio (It) – uncle.

zittella (It) – girl.

zivilstandsamt (Sz) – place for registration of vital statistics.

zoon (Du) – son.

zuigeling (Du) – infant.

zuster (Du) – sister.

Abbreviations of names
  and places . . . 12
Arranging your record . 48
Borrowing books . . . 103
Cache County Library . III
Catalogues, Library . . 102
Census Records . . . 107
Cleaning old photos . . 26
County Records . . . 123
County Histories . . . 120
County designations . . 80
Dates, approximating . 135
Dates, writing . . . 7
Dictionary 145
Everton, Walter M. . . III
Family group sheets . . I
Family histories,
  printed 98
Family history sheets . 42
Family traditions . . 71
Filing certificates . . 58
Foreign counties . . 80
Form letters . . . 33
Gaisford, Isaac . . . 61
Genealogical forms . XII
Gen. Helper . . IX, 89, 237
Genealogical libraries . 97
Genealogical record,
  numbering . . . 101
Genealogists' Check List
  and Historical Re-
  cords Survey . . 124
Genealogists' Exchange . IV
Genealogy takes time . 64
Handbook for Gene-
  alogical corres-
  pondence . . . 94

Handy Book For
  Genealogists . IV, X, 115

Historical Records
  Survey . . . . VI, 124
How To Begin 1
How To Continue . . . 55
Husbands, recording . . 14
Introduction to Handy
  Book 117
Jacobus, Donald Lines . . 82
Land Records 114

Letters, form . . . 85
Letters, where to write . 91
Letter Writing . . . 66, 83
Library Catalogues . . 102
Loose-leaf Binders . . 6
Many Errors . . . 60
Maps 122
Marriage, Family Group
  Sheet 13
Microfilming 52
Mimeograph, using . . 94
Names, clues in . . . 134
Names, persons with
  same 74
Names, spelling of . 74, 129
Names, whence came . 130
Names, writing . . . 8
National Archives . . 104
Naturalization
  Records 109
Numbering a Genealogical
  Record 101
Passenger Lists . . . 110
Pedigree chart . . . 27
Pedigree Charts, Listing
  names 35
Pedigrees, Correct . . 72
Personal History,
  writing 44
Personal Visits . . . 69

Persons of similar
   name 88
Picture Pedigrees . . 24
Pictures for your
   record 18
Place names 78
Printed Family
   Histories 98
Prove your work . . . 82
Rasmuson, Gunnar . . V
Registering your
   findings 56
Relationship Chart . . 138
Sample forms . . . 1
Sixth Ed. Handy Book
   for Genealogists . . 235
Spelling of Names . . 7, 129
Solving Discrepancies . 58
Sources of information,
   recording 17
State Histories . . . 119
Table of Contents . . . XIII
Ten Basic Steps in
   Genealogy 66
Traditions, Family . . 71
Truth, record 16
War Records 106
Where to Write . . . 91
Why a Genealogical
   Record 50
Wives, recording . . . 14
Writing Personal
   History 44

WHY YOU NEED
"THE HANDY BOOK FOR GENEALOGISTS"

"If I had had the "Handy Book" several years ago it would have saved me many long hours of research and answered thousands of questions I have had to dig out the hard way. Even now I find it to be one of the most used genealogical reference books I own." This was an unsolicited testimonial from a person who has done much professional research. Thousands of others have found this same help in their search for ancestors through information assembled in "The Handy Book for Genealogists" by George B. Everton, Sr.

The data contained therein is segregated and listed under the 50 States and most of the European countries. You are given a brief history of each; told when their vital records were started; where their records are kept; who to write to, etc. The counties of each state are listed with the county seat, date of organization, parent county, population, what census reports are available, their libraries and in many cases books are listed telling you where vital information may be obtained.

You will find a map of each state showing

their counties. As you begin research you will find it is extremely convenient to know what counties border the one you are working on and may give you a clue as to where to go next.

An example of how it may help you is the following: Your ancestor came from Hickman, Ky. which is the county seat of Fulton County. If you turn to page 86 in the "Handy Book" you find that Fulton County was formed in 1845 so all records since that time are found at Hickman. You also find Fulton was organized from Hickman, and Hickman was organized from Caldwell and Livingston in 1821; Caldwell from Livingston in 1809; Livingston from Christian in 1798; Christian from Logan in 1796; Logan from Lincoln in 1792; and Lincoln from Kentucky County Va. in 1780. You also find Kentucky County Va. was so designated in December 1776. You must go to the records of one or more of these other counties if your progenitor was there prior to 1845 and you can follow right on back for each change that was made almost pin-pointing the place you must look for his records. Send to THE EVERTON PUBLISHERS Inc., P.O. Box 368, Logan, Utah, 84321, for a free catalogue listing this book and many other research aids.

THE GENEALOGICAL HELPER

A bimonthly magazine published since 1947, has aided thousands of people all over the world. It is dedicated to "helping more people find more genealogy". It is not confined to any particular section of the country but serves people in every state and many foreign countries. It is edited and published by the same concern publishing this book, THE EVERTON PUBLISHERS, P.O. Box 368, Logan, Utah, 84321.

Hundreds of researchers have extended their pedigrees of many generations by utilizing the facilities offered in THE GENE-ALOGICAL HELPER. It is the most widely read genealogical magazine published. Send for a catalogue from THE EVERTON PUBLISHERS Inc., P.O. Box 368, Logan, Utah, 84321, listing the subscription price of the "Helper" and many other aids.